Computer Vision
A First Course

Artificial Intelligence Texts

Consulting Editors

T. ADDIS BSc, PhD
Department of Computer Science
University of Reading

B. DuBOULAY BSc, PhD, PCE
Centre for Cognitive Studies
University of Sussex
Brighton

A. TATE BA, PhD
Director
Artificial Intelligence Applications Institute
University of Edinburgh

Artificial Intelligence Texts

Computer Vision
A First Course

R.D. BOYLE BA, DPhil, MBCS
R.C. THOMAS BSc, MSc, MPhil
Department of Computer Studies
University of Leeds

Blackwell Scientific Publications
OXFORD LCNDON EDINBURGH
BOSTON PALO ALTO MELBOURNE

© 1988 by
Blackwell Scientific Publications
Editorial offices:
Osney Mead, Oxford OX2 0EL
  (*Orders:* Tel. 0865 240201)
8 John Street, London WC1N 2ES
23 Ainslie Place, Edinburgh EH3 6AJ
Three Cambridge Center, Suite 208,
  Cambridge, MA 02142, USA
667 Lytton Avenue, Palo Alto,
  California 94301, USA
107 Barry Street, Carlton
  Victoria 3053, Australia

First published 1988

Printed and bound in Great Britain by
Mackays of Chatham, Kent

DISTRIBUTORS

USA and Canada
  Blackwell Scientific Publications Inc
  PO Box 50009, Palo Alto
  California 94303
  (*Orders:* Tel. (415) 965-4081)

Australia
  Blackwell Scientific Publications
  (Australia) Pty Ltd
  107 Barry Street
  Carlton, Victoria 3053
  (*Orders:* Tel. (03) 347 0300)

British Library
Cataloguing in Publication Data

Boyle, R.D.
  Computer vision: a first course.
  1. Image processing
  I. Title
  006.4′2   TA1632

  ISBN 0–632–01577–2

Library of Congress
Cataloging-in-Publication Data

Boyle, Roger.
  Computer vision!

  Bibliography: p.
  Includes index.
  1. Computer vision.   I. Thomas, R. C.
  (Richard C.)
  II. Title
  TA1632.B69   1988   006.4′2   87–33860
  ISBN 0–632–01577–2

Contents

Preface

This is a book about Computer Vision. Computer Science is full of areas that are new and underexplained; Vision is one in which the problem is exacerbated since it brings together several disciplines. In the pages that follow, we shall touch on matters that may be categorised as Computer Science, Artificial Intelligence, Physics, Graphics, Engineering, Psychology, Physiology and Philosophy - Vision is a subject that is new and growing.

Many areas that we touch on are well (or better) established. Notably, Image Processing has been studied for many years now, particularly in the analysis of radiographs (X-rays) and satellite photographs, and Artificial Intelligence, a discipline with a short but distinguished history and a large literature. To attempt a definition of what we are trying to do is to invite criticism and complaint, but we may say that, while Image Processing takes an "image" (being deliberately vague about what the terms actually mean) and processes it for human viewing, and Graphics, on the basis of some "information", draws a picture, Vision will start with an "image" and "automatically" provide analysis for a subsequent decision. This requires an ability to perform all the tasks of Image Processing implicitly, but after that to search the image for features of use or interest, identify and locate objects, and consequently act. The "decision" or action may be to fire a missile, to move a robot arm on an assembly line, to reject a manufactured component in an inspection phase, to cause a mobile robot to change direction ... The scope is wide and we make no attempt to itemise all that we may wish to do.

Vision is difficult. This is not immediately obvious since it is a skill that we as humans take for granted; that we are so good at Vision leads many researchers to analyse our own visual perception in their attempts to build machine systems. Facetiously, *homo sapien* represents the only evidence we have that the Vision problem has a comprehensive solution. The "state of the art" is just a stage on the road to this solution. It will be clear that some of what we describe is well understood, and has been for years, while others aspects are still not fully explained and are the topics of debate in the research community. Accordingly, some references are to well established texts while others, equally worth following up, will be to recent journal literature.

This book is based on a third year optional course that we have taught at Leeds University since 1985, although we move beyond the undergraduate content at several points. It is written largely because of a perceived absence of books at the level of the advanced undergraduate or M.Sc. student. Vision has a number of authoritative texts, notably (Ballard & Brown,

1982, Marr 1982) and this volume is not intended to imply any shortcomings in them. Rather, we feel that they are aimed higher than this text; research publications are a useful and essential way forward, and all we are trying to do is bridge the gap. As a result of our standpoint and requirements, the book may have an unexpected profile for the Vision *cognoscente* - some things may appear to be laboured and some omitted. So be it; perhaps the laboured sections (if that is the reader's opinion) will make the subject easier to grasp, and when *Computer Vision: A Second Course* is produced the omissions will be corrected. We hope in passing that this book gathers together many useful references to work more recent than the authoritative texts.

Vision tasks are often categorised as *low*, *medium* or *high* level. Roughly, Chapter 1 in what follows is an overview and introduction, Chapters 3 and 4 are devoted to the low level tasks; Chapters 5, 7 and 8 are medium level, while 9 and 10 are high level. Chapter 6 presents a case study pointing out some uses of the algorithms and ideas described before. Without further knowledge of these categorisations, this information tells the reader nothing of course, and even when the terminology does mean something to you, you may quibble with the categories. It is intended though that the book be read "in order", as frequently material will assume knowledge of what has gone before. The exception to this is Chapter 2; this describes an existing pattern classification system which, while out of the main stream of Vision development, we find useful to describe since it is conceptually simple and at the same time (within its constraints) very powerful. It is a good way of showing what is possible *without* knowledge of the more abstruse ideas, and of defining what problems we might actually want to solve.

The Appendices serve to support the text at several points; in particular they cover some introductory Fourier theory which is not presented elsewhere, and look in detail at a particular Vision algorithm which we have found useful for teaching purposes. Most Chapters end with a selection of exercises of varying difficulty, whose solutions are also included as an Appendix.

At this point we could enumerate the topics covered, but perhaps it is more useful to state a caveat; this is a book from which a course can be taught. As such, it necessarily omits much and glosses over much else. Where this is the case, we hope that the relevant references are given to direct further reading, but we admit openly that several subjects (Gaussian based edge detectors, a study of motion, 3D modelling ..) are only mentioned in passing - this is after all a "First Course".

Various parts of this book owe a great debt to the lucid explanations of workers in Computer Vision and Artificial Intelligence in other books and journals. If our explanations bear a resemblance at any point to published literature, it is meant as a tribute to the original authors that we could not improve their presentation, and it is our intention that all such occurrences are credited in the text.

We should like here also to acknowledge the Department of Computer Studies at Leeds University for providing the environment in which this book was written, and our personal thanks are due to Boubeker Abdellouche, Maggie Boyle, Peter Dew, Phil Hobley, Lindsay Manning, Les Proll, Stuart Roberts, and Han Wang for their careful reading and perceptive comments on earlier drafts and general helpful advice. Any errors of fact or typography which remain are entirely the responsibility of the authors, who will be glad to incorporate corrections into future editions.

Roger Boyle
Richard Thomas
University of Leeds
October 31, 1987

CHAPTER 1

Perception 知觉

Human Perception

Computer Vision is hard. To see why, glance at Figure 1.1.

What did you see? It should be clear that it was a dinner table. It is not very difficult for humans because meal tables are an everyday item, and one glance is often sufficient to say what we are looking at. Humans appear to have a startling capacity to process visual information: Figure 1.1, which was digitised using a system outlined in Chapter 3, contains approximately 1/4Mbyte of data.

Let us consider the picture from the point of view of what Computer Vision systems need to be able to do if they are to rival human vision at all. The first point is the repetition: there are a number of discrete place settings each consisting of two plates, a glass, cutlery etc. As the place settings move in space, around the table, their orientation from the point of view of the viewer changes as does the shape of each item. For instance, circular plates become approximately elliptical at a angle in a clearly defined mathematical manner. Another point is that objects shrink in size with distance due to perspective, the mathematics of which will be familiar to those with a good grounding in computer graphics (Newman & Sproull, 1979).

The next point is vital to Computer Vision: some objects are hidden, or *occluded*, by others. The pattern of occlusion depends upon the *viewpoint* as well as the relative positions of the objects.

Careful examination of the plates shows various shading patterns in addition to their own design patterns, while the glasses have reflections in them. In fact, the reflections are very pronounced - to the objective viewer the "bright spots" due to the lighting are far more conspicuous than the object doing the reflecting.

Examine the picture again, this time in more depth, and notice the various irregularities such as spacings and orientations. There is also an oddity: of the three (visible) places set, one is laid left handed. The irregularity in the pattern can be explained quite quickly by the human viewer.

Notwithstanding all these pitfalls, we still feel able to mention the chair! Humans have an ability to fill in the missing parts of the picture, which in

1

Figure 1.1 A dinner table scene

this case may be fuelled by the expectation of chairs at the table.

Recognition

To recognise an object requires some prior imagery of it. Indeed there is a fascinating account of this by Gregory (Gregory 1978). A man in his fifties, blind from birth, had his sight restored by surgical techniques which had become practical for his case. After some time he was shown a simple lathe but completely failed to comprehend it even though he was interested in making things with hand tools. Once however he had put his hands over it, and *felt* it as he used to do when blind, he was able to *see* it, and said "Now that I've felt it I can see".

If the Computer Vision problem were merely to recognise or classify a scene from one of several candidates, for example a table set for breakfast, lunch, afternoon tea or dinner, then we could employ special purpose hardware as described in Chapter 2. This system is a remarkable achievement: it can be trained in literally a few seconds to discriminate between a small set of different scenes, for example people's faces. Its discrimination abilities far outweigh conventional Vision systems in respect of speed of both programming and operation; see for example the classic software experiment at learning structural descriptions of an object from examples (Winston 1975) is mentioned in Chapter 9. Problems with the special hardware approach occur if discrimination between larger sets of scenes is required. When there are several objects, each in any orientation and at any relative position, combinatorial explosion is rapidly encountered. This is a feature of most Artificial Intelligence problems! We have to cut down the search space through the deployment of knowledge such as perspective, and through the transformation of the original scene presented to the system, the *image*, into other compact representations.

Computer Vision

So Computer Vision is more than recognition. We are trying to build meaningful and explicit descriptions of physical objects from an image (Ballard & Brown, 1982).

The range of applications is growing rapidly. Robotics and inspection spring to mind, as do medicine, physics and chemistry. Traffic management, security and document processing are still in their infancy. Satellite and aerial photography is also a rich and established field.

Computer Vision is strongly interdisciplinary and has clear links, at a research level, with psychology, neurophysiology and philosophy.

Levels of Processing

It will be apparent from the discussion on human perception that processing takes place at several levels. On the one hand high level abstractions were needed to reason about the world of dinner tables, and on the other hand quite low level, normally subconscious, abilities appear to have been used to consider the shading on the plates. For Computer Vision a hierarchical approach is also adopted.

Low level routines perform tasks such as *edge detection*. An edge corresponds to to a sharp change in the brightness of an image, which in turn frequently corresponds to the boundary between two faces of an object, or between two objects. In Chapter 4 we shall meet some techniques for edge detection, and see some example figures; there are inherent problems in edge detectors, such as detecting more edges than one would intuitively expect.

There are many edge detection algorithms and it is a matter for skill and judgement to apply them in a particular application. Special purpose hardware can speed up this computationally intense procedure. It is curious to note that there is some evidence to suggest that similar edge detection processing may occur in the retina of primates (Winston 1984).

At a slightly higher processing level, the edges need to be refined into useful subsets which can be grouped together to form what can loosely be called the outlines of objects. In Chapter 5 we shall meet techniques for achieving this. A motivation for this boundary detection is that humans are often good at recognising objects from poor outlines; thus it is plausible that machines can reason in this mode.

A closely related problem is to find the regions within the boundary, and often region growing and boundary detection techniques co-operate to give a better *segmentation* of the image than either one alone. At this level of processing some application specific knowledge is often deployed; for example it may be known that an image only contains straight lines. Some techniques such as the widely used Hough transform can detect any parameterisable shape; example Figures in Chapter 6 will demonstrate how such features can be picked out directly.

Matching

We now have a representation of the image which is an abstraction away from the raw data, but it is still *viewer centred*, i.e. based on what the viewer or camera sees. Each of the various segments of the image is examined to find a plausible explanation in terms of the co-ordinate systems for particular objects. The output from this elaborate process is an object centred, or *world model*.

It has already been mentioned that to recognise something requires prior imagery and what is done in matching is to work backwards. A hypothesis that an object is in the scene is generated and then a search is performed to find a combination of orientation and viewpoint which gives a close approximation to the actual image. Matching can converge efficiently if the object has strong features. When dealing with geometrically well defined objects analytical techniques can be deployed. At other times more pragmatic rules of thumb are used, for example an object might be matched by its colour and image area. Whatever the method, matching is truly model based: segments of the image are matched against ideal models to give a world model of what the scene actually contains.

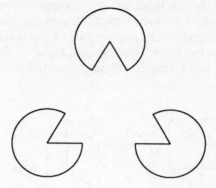

Figure 1.2 The triangle illusion

Ambiguity and Illusions

A major issue during the matching process is to decide which hypotheses to test and when. Very often assumptions will be made which later prove to be false or contradictory. Human vision performance suggests that there may be problems in this area which are intrinsically hard to solve. Take our ability to fill in gaps, for instance, which helped us to see the chair at the dining table. The same ability puts a triangle into Figure 1.2 where none exists. (It would be wrong to suggest that we have anything like a complete understanding of human visual perception. A notable attempt to explain what understanding we have is given by David Marr (Marr 1982) in a text to which we shall refer many times in this book.)

Figure 1.3 The railway line illusion

Another problem is the tendency to misapply deeply embedded rules. There is a whole class of pictures which humans perceive in a distorted way apparently due to inappropriate application of perspective heuristics. One such picture is the railway line illusion, see Figure 1.3, where the two horizontal bars are the same length although the bottom one is perceived as shorter.

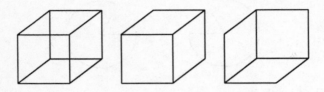

Figure 1.4 The Necker cube

Sometimes there is too little information to resolve contradictions. For example, the famous Necker cube, on the left of Figure 1.4, "flips" in the mind between the two possible interpretations shown alongside it - the brain is unsure which is correct and gives credence to both. (Recently Connectionist Machine architecture has been used to simulate this effect. (Rumelhart & McClelland 1986))

Occasionally what is seen does not square with reality. These so called impossible objects are a source of great amusement and even an art form. At first glance Figure 1.5 looks plausible, until the longer lines are carefully followed. We shall see in Chapter 7 that Computer Vision systems can be built that are not deceived by such objects.

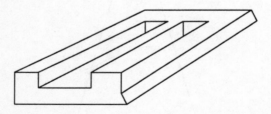

Figure 1.5 An impossible object

Primed with the above example an intelligent, adaptive system might now build into its rule base the notion of impossible objects. How could it then be sure all possible interpretations of an image had been explored?

What makes Figure 1.6 possible?

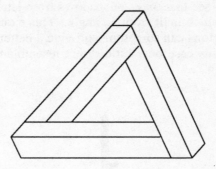

Figure 1.6 An impossible object?

The solution is to realise that the angles are not as they appear, but are actually as shown in Figure 1.7; we have been looking at a genuine three dimensional body, but from an angle that gives it a very odd appearance.

This shows how well the image that is seen is only a part of the world model. A Computer Vision system with comprehensive "depth data" (that is, knowledge of three dimensional co-ordinates of the image features) would have had no problem with this object, by the way.

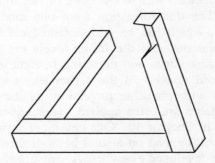

Figure 1.7 Explanation of the illusion

The perspective illusions, in particular, should help the reader to understand that some misinterpretations can be avoided if the pictures and figures are considered to be flat representations of a three dimensional world. As a final example, look at Figure 1.8.

For an explanation see Figure 1.9. The chain of reasoning is quite complex: once it is realised that the regions correspond to letters in some way, it becomes possible to see that they are shadows from letters formed by indentation of a surface which is lit from an angle. This example also happens to demonstrate that regions can sometimes provide a better perceptual clue that outlines, which in this case bear little direct resemblance to the letters and only hide the shading.

Figure 1.8 A familiar object

Conclusions

The major theme running through the book is that in order to see, a model of what is to be seen is required. The output from a Computer Vision system is a world model about objects and the relationships between them. The input to the system is a model, perhaps expressed as a comprehensive three dimensional description together with knowledge of the lighting properties and camera geometry. The transformation from one model to the other is a hierarchical process, which can be accomplished either bottom up or top down or even middle out. At the lower levels the processes deal with matters such as finding edges and detecting boundaries with the eventual output of a segmented image. At the higher levels there are attempts to match the segments with plausible projections of the objects; during this process ad-hoc heuristics are often applied. Techniques for integrating this process are covered in Chapter 10. One day more formal methods may be available, but they will depend on a solid basis of theory on visual perception, such as is being developed elsewhere (Leeuwenberg & Buffart, 1978).

Exercises

(1)   It is possible to categorise the purpose of most existing Vision systems as one of

Assembly

Inspection
Navigation
Recognition

List some examples of which you know, mentioning into which category you think they fall.

Draw some conclusions about the problems peculiar to each of these categories.

Figure 1.9 Shadow letters

CHAPTER 2

A Pattern Recognition System

It is useful at this stage to examine a functioning, commercially available pattern recognition system, just to give a feeling for what is possible before we start to apply any processing or reasoning algorithms. This Chapter describes a well known device which, while not representative of modern Vision apparatus, can readily be understood with little groundwork. The system to be described, named WISARD, was the culmination of many years of research work (Aleksander et al., 1984), some of which was spent waiting for appropriate technology to appear at reasonable prices. It is a very good example of an efficient *recognition* device, and that alone - WISARD does not pretend to have the capability to conduct precise image analysis; it is particularly interesting as its function is based on a model of the operation of neurons. It is an example of an *adaptive network*.

The system was first built in prototype form by its inventors, Igor Aleksander, John Stonham and Bruce Wilkie, at Brunel University in 1981; it is now marketed by Computer Recognition Systems[*] of Wokingham, England. WISARD derives its name from its more cumbersome title; **WI**lkie, **Ston**ham and **Aleksander's** **R**ecognition **D**evice.

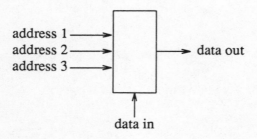

Figure 2.1 A simple RAM

Before describing the way a full WISARD system operates, a small example of the principles involved will be presented. It is necessary to take

[*]Computer Recognition Systems Ltd, Unit 3, Fishponds Close, Fishponds Road, Wokingham, Berkshire, RG11 2QA, UK.

for granted at this stage that a "scene" - whatever natural world pattern it is that we wish to recognise - can be represented by a lattice of zeroes and ones. These ideas will be presented in greater detail in the next chapter, but it should be intuitively clear that a binary (black/white) image can be derived by imagining a grid being placed in front of a scene and entering a 1 in squares that are "bright" and a 0 in others. Considerations of what is "bright", and what the grid resolution might be, are not strictly relevant here and are delayed until the next chapter.

The description of the ideas behind WISARD that follows is based heavily on the original papers (Aleksander & Stonham, 1978) whose clarity is here acknowledged. The interested reader is recommended to look up the primary references.

1	1	1
0	1	0
0	1	0

Figure 2.2 An ideal ''T''

A Simple Example

Suppose we have at our disposal a random access memory (*RAM*) device with 3 address lines, a one bit data-out line and a one bit data-in line; each address points to one bit of memory. In *read mode* one of $2^3=8$ 3-bit addresses will be applied to the address lines, and the data-out line will generate whatever the RAM holds at that address. In *write mode* the contents of the location currently addressed are set to whatever is applied to the data-in line. Figure 2.1 shows this schematically.

Suppose that our "scene" is digitised into a binary, 3×3 grid, and that we hope to recognise an upper case T. An ideal T is illustrated in Figure 2.2. Of course, there is a total of 2^9 *possible* patterns here since each of the nine bits may be 0 or 1. We now allocate these bits to the address lines of some RAMs - we can use three RAMs, each of which is addressed by three of the bits in the binary image; one assignment of bits to RAMs might be on a horizontal row basis as in Figure 2.3, although other allocations may turn out to be suitable in due course.

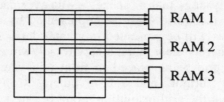

Figure 2.3 Row by row address allocation

First of all we *teach* the RAMs about the pattern we wish to recognise; a (relatively) small set of T-like patterns is shown to the RAMs - the idea is that we let the system know that a T may not be "perfect" in the sense of Figure 2.2, and that "near misses" (not all of which need to be seen explicitly in advance) are probably admissible. Suppose the teaching set of images is a perfect T, and the two slightly corrupted T's of Figure 2.4. For teaching, the RAMs are erased to 0, and then put into write mode with the data-in lines held to 1. Each member of a teaching set is then shown to the system. The effect is that "good" patterns have the corresponding RAM addresses set to 1, while others are kept at 0. After teaching, the RAM contents, in addresses 0 to 7 respectively, are given in Table 2.1.

Table 2.1

	0	1	2	3	4	5	6	7
RAM 1	0	0	0	0	0	0	1	1
RAM 2	0	0	1	1	0	0	0	0
RAM 3	1	0	1	0	0	0	0	0

1	1	0
0	1	1
0	1	0

1	1	1
0	1	0
0	0	0

Figure 2.4 Slightly corrupt "T"'s

After teaching, the RAMs are put into read mode, and we can hold test patterns up to them; consider what happens when they are shown Figure 2.5. The first RAM is addressed at (binary) 110, the second at 010 and the third at 010; looking back at the teaching phase, we see that each RAM will now provide a 1 on its data-out line - if we choose to sum these outputs, the "score" of the test pattern is 3 out of a potential maximum of 3. The system assesses the test pattern as a very likely T, even though it has never seen the pattern before. Conversely, if it is shown Figure 2.6 the RAMs are addressed at 101, 111 and 101 respectively, and will provide a sum "score" of 0. The system has said that the pattern is very far from what it has been taught about - the correct conclusion.

1	1	0
0	1	0
0	1	0

Figure 2.5 A test "T"

1	0	1
1	1	1
1	0	1

Figure 2.6 An unlikely "T"

Notice that in recognition mode, we are applying some function to the RAM data out lines; in the example above we took their arithmetic sum and regarded it as a "score" - other options are logical AND, logical OR or, perhaps, *weighted* sums. There are many ways of constructing criteria for acceptance or rejection of test patterns.

The idea being mimiced here is that of a model (McCulloch & Pitts, 1943) of brain neurons. It is thought that neurons "fire" at their output (axon) when certain configurations of their "inputs" (synapses) fire; exactly which configurations cause the firing is a question of learning. The similarity with our simple RAM should now be clear - to fire or not to fire is a simple binary condition that supplies the 1 or 0 on the RAM output. McCulloch and Pitts proposed the mathematical model illustrated in Figure 2.7. Various inputs I_i are weighted by fixed weights w_i and summed; the result is then compared with a fixed threshold t and a binary output generated accordingly. It is easy to see that the toy system described above uses ideas that are a generalisation of this idea, and is thus, at a very trivial level, an attempt to mimic the brain's own learning mechanism. Like the brain, we have a system that ''learns'' from being shown some demonstration patterns and is capable of generalisation; it is not, though, dependent on a Von Neumann structure. There is no central processor storing the input information in a kind of ''filing cabinet'' - rather, a very large collection of primitive cells adapts itself into a state of ''knowing''.

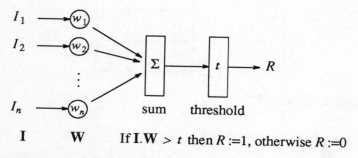

$$\text{If } \mathbf{I.W} > t \text{ then } R := 1, \text{ otherwise } R := 0$$

Figure 2.7 The McCulloch-Pitts neuron model

The WISARD System

WISARD uses exactly the same ideas as the three RAM system described above, but on a larger scale. The RAMs are very similar, but normally have four address lines and the images handled are up to 512 bits square. The total number of bits in the image is thus $512 \times 512 = 262144$, and the total number of RAMs required to ensure that each image bit is used on (exactly) one address line is $262144/4 = 65536$ - the allocation of image bits to RAMs is random, unlike the systematic scheme used in the T example. The output ''function'' applied to the RAMs is simple summation, giving a maximum ''score'' of 65536 for a pattern. Interestingly, the recognition powers of the system improve only slightly with increasing the number of address lines to a RAM - there is no virtue in using more than four or five.

Such a setup has conspicuous success at tasks such as face recognition - if a particular face is shown to the system in about 300 (frontal) positions, then subsequent images of the same face will "score" 95% or more of the maximum response, while other faces will score much less. In practice, of course, we want such a setup to distinguish between a number of different faces. We can achieve this by providing a set of RAMs and an image to address line correspondence for each such face - WISARD calls such a RAM set and address correspondence a *discriminator*. Each discriminator is then taught on a different face, and each test image is compared with each of the discriminators - that which provides the maximum response, if this maximum is larger than some reasonable threshold (such as 95%), is deemed to be the correct classification. Such a scheme has obvious applications in recognising letters, which would require twenty six discriminators.

As a measure of how successful the system is, we can observe (Stonham 1983) that it has been used successfully with two discriminators to distinguish between the same face smiling and frowning. Other live applications of the system have been in bank note recognition (distinguishing between notes of different denomination and nationality) and post-code reading. Many other tasks which are essentially *classification* suggest themselves.

Efficiency

The machine as marketed does not in fact consist of large numbers of RAMs with four bits addressing one other bit, although the principle of the system is indeed as described. We can observe that a 1-megabit memory (with 20 bit addresses) can be used as follows; the first four bits can be assigned to the data input and so correspond to the four address bits described above; this leaves sixteen unused, which can be used as an index into up to 65536 ($=2^{16}$) different assignments of image bits to address lines - the one memory chip can thus be used to construct a discriminator for a 512×512 image as described earlier.

Further, if the RAM addresses K-bit words instead of single bits, it can be used as K different discriminators; the cost of such memory chips is now extremely low, although this was not always the case. Indeed, the ideas behind WISARD were developed by the Brunel team before the cost of the components was low enough to make building the device viable.

A block diagram of the WISARD hardware is shown in Figure 2.8. Here we suppose the image is stored in the frame buffer as a 512 square array of bits; this array is addressed by an 18-bit "map generator" which, subject to a clock CL1, cycles through the bits selecting them in the order that the randomly assigned 4-tuples are expecting them. These bits are clocked serially by CL3 into a four bit long shift register where, when four bits have been

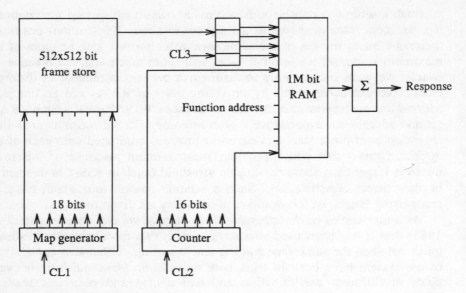

Figure 2.8 WISARD hardware

collected, they are used as an index into a one megabit RAM. The remaining sixteen bits of the RAM address are selected by a counter, controlled by another clock (CL2); this counter represents the address of the "4-tuple function" currently under inspection. In read mode, the one bit output generated by this composite address is added to a counter; in write mode the selected address would be set to one.

The speed of the device is also relevant; access times on such RAMs will be less than 50 nanoseconds (5×10^{-8} seconds), so serially accessing 65536 locations will take less than $65536 \times 5 \times 10^{-8}$ seconds, or 3.3 milliseconds. This compares very favourably with the time taken to capture a TV image, which typically refreshes in forty milliseconds, meaning that the teaching and discrimination phase can be conducted in real time, that is, by holding the relevant scene in front of a TV camera. The "face learning" exercise that precedes face recognition thus needs a subject to be in front of a TV camera for as long as it takes to collect about 300 frames - approximately 12 seconds - which represents very good performance indeed.

Observations

WISARD is an interesting system, distinguished by having demonstrated its abilities over some considerable time and being a successful commercial product. It is also unusual as Vision systems go since it has no "understanding" of what it is looking at; it has no model of the objects it is supposed to recognise, and indeed no mechanism to reconstruct a perfect example of that for which it is looking. Given the toy, 3×3 system used to search for the letter T earlier, we could not, after the learning phase, construct a T by looking at the contents of the memories ands asking what the WISARD was trying to recognise. On the other hand, it *can*, very accurately, assess whether a pattern it has never seen before resembles anything it has been taught about.

The memories, of course, never store a copy of the input images, or anything that could be reconstructed into one. As such, WISARD can only be used as a *classification* aid - it can answer questions such as "Does this image resemble anything about which you have been taught", and can give a measure of how good any such a resemblance is. The value of the measure is not, though, easy to determine - if one discriminator gives a response of 89% while another gives a response of 91%, we have no way of measuring how reliably "better" the second is than the first - an inadequate training phase could well give rise to weak responses. In practice, however, this rarely seems to occur - one response is usually far better than all the others.

Further, while WISARD does recognise patterns, it knows nothing of their structure; a discriminator trained on the face of Gustav Mahler would recognise it very well in a number of expressions or distortions until it was turned upside down, after which it would give a very low response - the WISARD only knows about what it has been taught about, and rotation is something it cannot be taught about (at least, not explicitly). Likewise, if it were shown a different face, the response may be (relatively) either high or low, but it would not be able to say "Yes, this is a face, but not one I have seen before" - the new picture may just as well be of a wheelbarrow.

This becomes a serious deficiency when we need to identify objects in images with precision; if we want to recognise, for example, circles or straight edges, or know the distance of an object from the camera, or locate it precisely in space for robot manipulation, WISARD cannot help, and much of the rest of this book is about how such problems can be approached. Inspection tasks are usually concerned with questions such as "How many faulty threads can I see in this textile sample? What is their density; their average length and breadth?" or "Is the correct number of holes drilled in this component? Are they in the correct positions, and of the correct diameter?" Questions such as this need answering with precision; WISARD could certainly recognise a component with *approximately* the right holes, in *approximately* the correct places, but not at the tolerance level demanded by industrial assembly processes.

These observations should not detract from the efficiency, skill and speed with which WISARD functions as a classifier. WISARD functions as a *single layer network*; it is in active use in several places, notably Brunel University where it was first developed, as a research tool. One particular project is to develop the ideas into use of *multi level* networks, in which the discrimination between patterns is subject to refinement when ambiguities arise - for example in trying to distinguish between the letter ''C'' and the letter ''O'', which have considerable similarities when digitised. It turns out that WISARDs connected serially, so that one interprets the patterns output by another, have even more powerful pattern recognition properties (Stonham et al., 1987, Kani & Wilson, 1987). That the underlying theory is based on attempts to understand the brain's own pattern classification techniques makes WISARD all the more interesting as an experimental tool.

Exercises

(1) Examine the example 3×3 ''discriminator'' in the text, and determine the ''score'' that would be generated for each of the test patterns shown in Figure 2.9. How is the score affected if, instead of being formed by a summation, it is
   (i) A logical AND of the RAM outputs.
   (ii) A logical OR of the RAM outputs.

1	1	1
1	1	1
1	1	1

0	1	1
1	1	0
0	1	0

1	1	1
0	1	1
0	1	0

Figure 2.9 Example test patterns

(2) Examine the example in the text, and list all 3×3 patterns that give a maximum response to the 3 RAM ''discriminator'' described. What happens to this set if the RAM addresses are selected from *vertical* rows, rather than horizontal?

(3) Examine the example in the text; how many patterns score *one less* than the maximum
   (i) with the horizontal allocation of bits to RAMs as described?
   (ii) when the ''score'' of a test pattern is calculated by adding *twice* the output of RAM 1 to the outputs of the other two RAMs (forming a *weighted* sum in the sense of the McCulloch-Pitts

neuron model).

What characterises these ''one offs' in the second case?

(4)   Randomly reconnect the RAM addresses to image cells in the T example, and determine whether the resulting system discriminates for the T patterns in the text as well as the regular connection used.

CHAPTER 3

Image Acquisition and Modelling

Television Pictures

It is easy to take our ability to see for granted: we forget what wonderful instruments our eyes are, and do not often marvel at the workings of our brains. In order for Computer Vision to occur at all we need to start with the equivalent of an eye. The most obvious example is a television camera, whose output is a video signal.

The broadcast television image we see is a very crude representation of a scene. It is a continuous analogue signal with a periodicity which represents a sequence of frames of 625 horizontal lines; in order to improve viewing comfort, each frame has two sequential fields made up of alternative scan lines (see Figure 3.1). A field is broadcast in 1/50 second in Europe and some other parts of the world (in the USA the standard is 525 lines and 1/60 second), meaning that it takes 1/25 second to transmit a complete frame, or 40 frames per second. This gives some idea of the rate at which real time applications (such as the WISARD learning phase discussed in Chapter 2) will have to perform their computation, if they derive their input from this sort of technology.

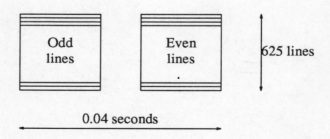

Figure 3.1 A TV frame

We do not see the image flicker because it persists in the eye for a short time: the interlacing of the two fields of the frame is designed to

20

complement and exploit this natural characteristic.

The definition of the image is a measure of how much information it can contain. Clearly the number of lines per frame is important, but so too is the rate at which the intensity of the image can vary along each line. A third factor is the range of intensity levels that the image can take at any point, the lowest being binary. Measurement is a complex area (Pearson 1975).

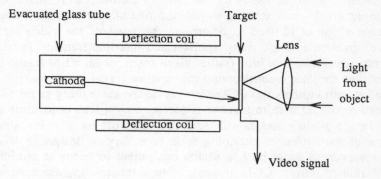

Figure 3.2 A vidicon tube

Television cameras fall into two broad classes: thermionic and, in recent years, solid-state. A cheap and effective thermionic device is the vidicon tube shown schematically in Figure 3.2.

The scene is focused on the target by means of the lens. The target is scanned, in frame fashion, by an electron beam generated by the cathode and focused by the magnetic fields induced by currents in the deflection coils. The cathode has to be hot and at a negative potential with respect to the target, and the glass tube needs to contain a vacuum, in order to work. The current at the target depends upon the intensity of light incident upon it. This current is tapped for a video signal that can subsequently be reconstructed to depict the scene originally incident on the target.

Inherent in such a device are several distorting factors. The target has a tendency to suffer from image persistence of several seconds: this can easily be observed when a camera is moved rapidly from one scene to another in such a manner that the first image gradually fades away. Also the target does not have a linear performance over the whole spectrum so that certain colours produce brighter images than others. In addition, an image can become burnt onto the target and spatial accuracy is often impaired because the deflection coils do not produce a completely linear scan of the target.

These problems can be addressed, sometimes at the expense of size and ruggedness, by more costly devices such as the image orthicon tube, but solid-state technology points the way to the future. The charge-coupled device (CCD) consists of an $n \times m$ array of photosensitive elements each of which produces an analogue output proportional to the amount of light incident on it. Such devices have advantages over thermionic devices in all the areas so far mentioned, plus power consumption and sensitivity. They are also versatile; a simple use is for the array of elements to be scanned by clocking logic row by row starting in position one of row one; the value of each element's output is used to determine the level of the video signal. Alternative arrangements are frame transfer and interline transfer, in which the elements are clocked *en bloc* (either all of them, or on a line basis) into separate storage for later reconstruction into a video signal.

Logically, both vidicon and CCD cameras do the same thing as far as the user is concerned - light from a scene is focussed by a lens onto some surface (the *image plane*) and is subsequently read off as a video signal. Knowledge of the different technologies is necessary in designing Vision systems, however, in order best to match equipment to needs at minimum cost. As a rule of thumb, CCD devices, as new technology, are becoming relatively cheaper and of better quality. Monochrome vidicon cameras may be obtained for about £200 at cheapest, with quality and colour costing more; good quality monochrome CCD cameras are coming onto the market at the time of writing for about £500.

Digitisation Techniques

The output from a TV camera will conform to a standard (CCIR 1971). A device called a *frame buffer* or *frame grabber* is often employed to take the analogue TV signal and digitise it into discrete picture elements, or *pixels*, for subsequent transfer to computer memory.

A fairly typical laboratory setup which employs a frame buffer is shown in Figure 3.3. The frame buffer has adequate RAM to store (at least) one digitised image. Normally the RAM is updated in real time and its contents can be dumped into workstation memory at any time by DMA on receipt of a suitable command from the software. In addition the buffer contents may be continually reconverted into analogue form, or rasterised, for display on the TV monitor. In certain modes of operation the monitor can also be used to display images stored or processed by the workstation. Images reproduced in this book come from just such a system.

In the configuration shown, the buffer memory exists on a series of one or more *planes* which can be combined to give red, green and blue outputs, and provide a colour image; the memory of the buffer is mapped into the

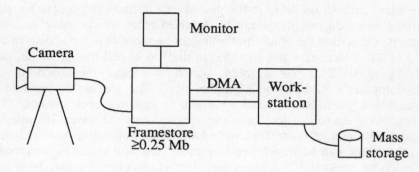

Figure 3.3 A laboratory setup

address space of the workstation and thus appears as a memory "extension", facilitating very fast access.

Another feature is the optional provision of special purpose hardware on the system bus for the execution of certain low level algorithms. If such hardware is available then various algorithms can be applied to images that would otherwise need to use the workstation processor; this can result in image transformations being effected at very high speed, often in real time. To the human viewer this has the effect of displaying *processed* images with no apparent delay.

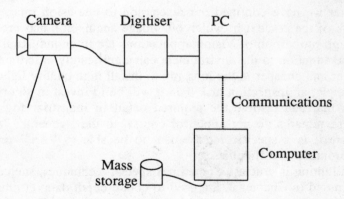

Figure 3.4 A simple laboratory setup

The main point about a frame buffer is that real time, or video rate, digitisation occurs given sufficient hardware. Serious study of, for example, motion in images will demand this sort of facility, but any application that requires regular collection of images will eventually come to depend on there being little or no delay in the procedure. If, however, cost is a serious consideration then the image can be digitised more slowly using an image scanner; in this case the configuration might be more like that shown in Figure 3.4. The electronics are arranged to digitise in real time a single, pixel wide, vertical slice of a field which is then transferred to the microcomputer's RAM using a parallel port. The process is repeated for successive adjacent slices until an entire image has been created. This method is satisfactory if the scene can remain static for about five seconds, although setting up the camera can be laborious. Following such a digitisation, the image can be transferred to a more powerful machine for processing; such an operation is tedious and time consuming, but has been used with some success as a cheap way of capturing a variety of images, although one is severely limited by the constraints of the system. The cost of the digitising apparatus (camera etc.) for this simple setup is somewhat less than £500 (Sterling), whereas the cost of a frame buffer and accessories will be considerably more. Buffers to attach to, for example, an IBM PC may be around £2000, while high quality buffers, with multiple memory planes, colour mappers and other accessories will start at about £10,000 - you get what you pay for! (Prices of this sort of apparatus fluctuate as fast as those of other computer hardware).

Image Acquisition as Part of a System

So far we have confined our discussion to television images. We need to think of the context in which our image acquisition and processing occurs. A high proportion of Vision applications are in an industrial context, where some attention to the environment can significantly ease the task - it will be easier and cheaper in the long run to install high quality lighting around, for example, an inspection task than it will be to invest in algorithms and cameras that can resolve the required detail in industrial fog, mist and dirt. These remarks do not apply, of course, to the "general" Vision problem, where it is a specific requirement to be able to "see" regardless of the environmental difficulties.

Lighting is crucial. Sometimes special techniques, such as light striping discussed in Chapter 8, are used to obtain depth data; at other times it may be necessary to use a special light source such as a laser or employ colour filters. In a production environment consistency is important, for example; will the level of ambient light be the same in winter and summer? will the wrapping on say, a chocolate bar, reflect light in unpredictable ways? could there be air turbulence due to high temperature gradients which causes distortion of the image?

It is also necessary and sometimes very intellectually rewarding to consider different ways of reaching a given design goal. In an automated inspection task the time required to process the image may appear large in relation to the speed at which items are presented to the camera. One solution is to make the Image Processing algorithms and hardware faster. However, once it is appreciated that the results of the inspection may not be required until the item has reached some point downstream in the production process, then it becomes possible to have cheaper, slower hardware working in parallel (Batchelor 1985).

The movement of a production line may also mean that a line-scan camera can be deployed instead of the conventional area-scan device. The complete image is created by the concatenation of lines scanned at regular time intervals as the item moves along the conveyor belt. This principle of letting the object move is taken to an extreme in satellite imagery: LANDSAT has a scanner that captures six horizontal lines at a time with vertical movement of the scan down the image achieved by the rotation of the earth. Images are recorded in four spectral bands, each of which is used to highlight certain features such as water, cities or vegetation.

Some Vision systems do not operate in the visible spectrum at all. Flaws in the interior of composite materials can be detected by applying heat to a surface and measuring the temperature profile at another place at regular intervals of time (Durrani et al., 1986). High resolution infra-red scanners are employed to drive a normal frame buffer, and hence some conventional algorithms are used for analysis.

We shall see in due course that multiple images of an object provide valuable additional information. Some very elaborate systems take pictures from a variety of different angles, which can be combined to "see inside" things. A well known example is the body scanner which is X-ray based (Gordon et al., 1975).

The trick in using a body scanner as a diagnostic tool is to know what to look for. This illustrates the difference between low level and high level Computer Vision techniques; low level algorithms produce the processed image, but high level knowledge is required to interpret it. Eventually one would expect at least some of this interpretation task to be performed by expert systems. In less sensitive applications, such as product inspection, the expert system element is often already embedded into the Vision system.

It is worth mentioning that it is expensive to measure items accurately using Computer Vision techniques. One method which can measure some surfaces down to a few microns is to use phase rather than intensity information about Moiré fringes. The image seen by the camera comprises bands of high and low intensity, similar to an aerial view of a ploughed field. The distance between the bands can be input into a fairly simple expression to compute the depth, however the approach has limitations when steep slopes are measured. Here too the effective use of vision depends upon consideration of the system as a whole.

Readers of this book are probably not going to be using highly sophisticated image acquisition equipment. Nevertheless, in any experimental setup it is always worth investing time in making the lighting and contrast as favourable as possible, and eliminating as much noise and reflection as possible, thereby minimising the image "restoration" that the software has to achieve. Ten minutes invested in setting the experiment up correctly can save hours in development of sophisticated filters at a later stage.

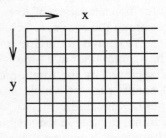

Figure 3.5 A digitisation lattice

The Image Model

By some means or other, we presume that we are presented with a digitised image; whether this is produced by a conventional vidicon camera, CCD device, heat sensor or any other mechanism is not particularly important here. The distinctive feature on which to focus is that we have generated a *two dimensional* image - in the majority of cases this will imply a rectangular, or more probably square, image, subdivided into a regular lattice of square pixels such as that in Figure 3.5. There is an obvious x,y coordinatisation of this grid; it is conventional in Image Processing for the origin to be at the top left of the image, as shown. Each pixel will have an associated grey level, and the image may thus be easily represented as a rectangular integer matrix.

It is worth observing at this stage that such a tessellation of the plane may not always be the best possible. Suppose, for example, we have an image of a black object containing a hole on a white background - its digitisation may then appear something like Figure 3.6. Now when, in due course, we come

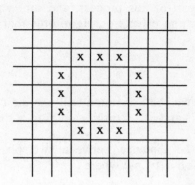

Figure 3.6 A digitised object

to ask how many "regions" this picture contains, the answer depends on which pixels we regard as connected to other pixels. If we admit only orthogonal connectivity (vertices "connected" only to their horizontal and vertical neighbours), the image represents four regions and, implicitly, four objects. If on the other hand we allow diagonally "connected" pixels to be called adjacent, then we have only one black object, but the interior of the hole is now connected to the exterior! The problem is not wholly facetious; a different tessellation, of triangles for instance, would not have provided this problem.

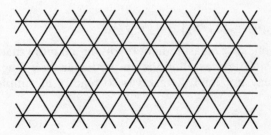

Figure 3.7 A triangular tessellation

If the object of our processing were just *Image Processing* these quirks would probably not matter; the end result of the exercise, an image somehow manipulated for human viewing, would not be much affected by such considerations. Vision, however, will be looking for automatic recognition of objects, their boundaries and holes. Location and identification of regions will be an important part of this process, and subtle problems just such as this may have far reaching effects on algorithms that follow early processing.

Distance in Images

Many algorithms that we shall examine will use the concept of "distance" between a pair of pixels and it is worth examining at this point what is meant by the term.

We shall expect the distance between two pixels p_1 and p_2 to be represented by a function $d(p_1,p_2)$ where

$$d(p,p) = 0$$

$$d(p_1,p_2) = d(p_2,p_1)$$

$$d(p_1,p_2) \leq d(p_2,p_3) + d(p_1,p_3)$$

- the usual definition of a *metric* (Bryant 1985). For the rectangular tessellation, a natural definition for pixels $p_1 = (x_1,y_1)$ and $p_2 = (x_2,y_2)$ is

$$d(p_1,p_2) = \sqrt{(x_1-x_2)^2+(y_1-y_2)^2}$$

the normal Euclidean distance metric. Bearing in mind that such an operation may need to be performed several thousand times for the sake of one algorithm it is clear that this metric, involving two multiplications and a square root, is potentially an expensive measurement. A different possibility may be

$$d(p_1,p_2) = |x_1-x_2| + |y_1-y_2| \qquad\qquad 3.1$$

a cruder but far cheaper measurement involving no more than additions.

Notice that different tessellations, in particular the triangular tessellation of Figure 3.7 may not lend themselves so readily to simple metric definitions.

Image Sizes

We shall assume henceforward that our images are composed of square pixels; indeed in most examples it is fair and reasonable to assume that the image itself is square. Normally it will be found that if an image is a square of length N pixels, then $N=2^n$ for some n - it should be no surprise that hardware generates data with "power-of-2" dimensions. Usually, images generated by image capturing equipment are at least 256 pixels square, and images 1024 or more pixels square are common.

Each pixel will represent a grey level in the range 0 to $M-1$ for some M where in all probability $M=2^m$ for some m; the common values of m are 1 (binary images), 8 (providing 256 distinct grey levels, requiring one byte per pixel storage) and 16 (providing 65636 grey levels, requiring two bytes per pixel). It is interesting to observe that when it comes to viewing a display of a scene, the human eye cannot distinguish between more than about thirty or forty grey levels (requiring only five bits of storage); algorithms for generating hard copy display may thus be appreciably simplified.

It should be clear by now that the storage requirements for images are going to be high; the table shows storage demands in 8 bit bytes for some example image dimensions.

Table 3.1

	Side length in pixels (square image) (N)		
M	32	256	1024
256 grey levels	1024	65536	1048576
65536 grey levels	2048	131072	2097152

It might be observed that ''A picture is worth a thousand words'', but we see here that a 256-grey level, 1024-square image needs a megabyte, or half a million 16-bit words, of storage space; the cost of this in both memory requirements and disk performance is high. Any Vision or Image Processing application will have demands for large numbers of images, and the implied demand for disk storage and rapid access is therefore large. More serious is that, however simple a given algorithm may be, it will be working on considerable quantities of data and it will, in terms of time, be accordingly expensive. Efficiency is provided by demanding that images reside in memory during processing - the virtual address spaces of modern processors mean that this is no problem, but ideally the image resides in *physical* memory to save paging time, and suddenly the image applications are seen to need powerful, preferably single user machines with considerable memory provision. This observation is doubly true when we consider that high quality display, both interactive and hard copy, is also desirable.

A fashionable solution to computing load problems is to use multi or parallel processors. Many of the algorithms to be presented in due course lend themselves to architectures that can exploit high degrees of parallelism (Dew and Manning, 1987); multi-processor systems may be expected to save time and per-processor memory requirements.

Colour

It is increasingly common for images to be acquired in colour; few specific mentions will be made in this book of algorithms that exploit colour, but frequently it may be taken for granted that they generalise easily.

Human colour perception is extremely complicated, but grossly simple ideas seem quite adequate for machines to produce good colour images. A colour image will probably be represented as a superimposition of three "primary" images - one red, one blue and one green, it being well known that (nearly) all colours can be synthesised from an appropriate combination of these three. This is also the way that most colour display devices will produce colour screen images. It should be observed, however, that other coordinatisations of colour space exist - best known are *IHS* (Intensity, Saturation and Hue) and *IQY* (Ballard & Brown, 1982). Both of these define a three dimensional colour space, and indeed, both are transformations of the Red, Green, Blue (*RGB*) "coordinates".

A good summary of current approaches to work in colour, especially related to inspection tasks, appears in (Thomas & Connolly, 1986)

Exercises

(1)   There is a wide range of Image Processing and Vision equipment on the market. What criteria would you use in selecting components of;
>   *(i)* A general purpose laboratory system.
>   *(ii)* A robot navigation system.
>   *(iii)* A system designed to inspect paintwork quality on a motor car assembly line.

(2)   Suggest a coordinate scheme for the plane tessellation shown in Figure 3.7, and provide a metric on this tessellation.

(3)   For a metric d on discrete 2D space, fixed point **a** and real number r, describe the "disk" defined by

$$d(\mathbf{a},\mathbf{x}) \leq r$$

when d is;
>   *(i)* The Euclidean metric and the space is quantised in square pixels.
>   *(ii)* The metric of equation 3.1 and the space is quantised in square pixels.
>   *(iii)* The metric defined in answer to the previous question, and the space is quantised in triangular pixels.

(4)   For storage purposes, image are often compressed. A well known technique is *run length encoding* in which we suppose an image is

stored row by row, and we devise a scheme in which long runs of pixels of the same intensity level are compressed to a pixel count, and the appropriate grey level. Design and implement a run length encoder (and decoder) and measure its space saving performance on some sample images.

Why are such schemes rarely part of "live" Image Processing or Vision systems?

(5) List some Image Processing or Vision applications in which the use of colour would be indispensable (or, at least, very valuable).

CHAPTER 4

Low Level Processing

In an ideal world images would be presented to algorithms in a perfect state, but this is rarely true in practice. There are two principle reasons why the image may be unsatisfactory - either it suffers from *noise* or it fails to highlight the particular feature in which we are interested. Any process that attempts to digitise the real world is prone to noise; image acquisition may find its data corrupted by the digitising equipment or by subsequent transmission. Even if noise is absent, or is somehow processed out, the resulting image may not emphasise what we want to see; good examples of this are underwater photographs or medical radiographs (X-rays) - in both cases the picture is of a scene that is itself "murky" in the sense that the underwater object we wish to see may be hidden by silt in suspension, or the bone or organ we wish to examine is unevenly occluded by varying depths of tissue.

Generally both problems are present and a number of techniques exist for *filtering* images to remove or at least partially suppress them. The algorithms we describe in this chapter are pure Image Processing and represent ideas that have been in use for some time; they are still necessary preliminaries to the Vision algorithms that follow. It is possible that the priorities are altered; noise suppression is useful to human viewers since the noise offends the eye - provided that noise does not corrupt or hide essential features, it is possible that machine algorithms may not demand its removal. Likewise, enhancement filters for machine algorithms may highlight sharp edges at the cost of concealing other features irrelevant to the machine that the human eye may depend on for recognition. The principles remain the same, though.

Elementary Noise Reduction

Much progress in cleaning noise can be made by making some simple assumptions about the character of the noise and the nature of the uncorrupted image. It is, for instance, reasonable to assume that the noise is randomly distributed with zero mean, causing pixel grey levels to be distorted randomly above and below their true values. There are circumstances in which this may not be the case; if the noise is known to behave in a different

32

way then other ideas must be used to clean it - without some analytic knowledge of its behaviour no more can be said here (see Exercise 4.2). In fact, noise frequently manifests itself as "spikes" - very small areas, perhaps only one pixel, that are significantly (i.e. visibly) corrupt. These may appear as white dots in a dark region, or black dots in a light region.

Another assumption may be that the pixels in a neighbourhood of a given pixel will have the same (or close) grey level in the clean image. This is not so easily justified; it will clearly be untrue near sharp edges or for large "neighbourhoods", but it does allow the definition of a simple noise-reducing filter.

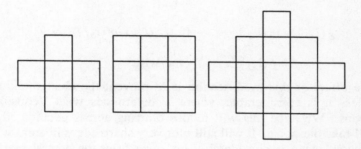

Figure 4.1 Sample windows

To clean a given pixel, we first define a *window W*, probably centred at that pixel; the window may well be a square (of odd length side) but may instead, for example, be a cross formed by the pixel and its four orthogonal neighbours. Assume it contains *w* pixels (probably including the "target" pixel). Now writing $f(i,j)$ for the original corrupted image and $g(i,j)$ for the cleaned image, we may say

$$g(i,j) = \frac{1}{w} \sum_{(n,m) \in W} f(n,m)$$

(that is, summing the grey values of the pixels in the window, and dividing by the number of such pixels) thus forming the *local average* grey level.

This filter is simple to implement and has the very desirable property that if an area of image is of uniform intensity and uncorrupted, then it remains so after the algorithm has passed. Clearly it will also damp down spikes which will be influenced by their less distorted neighbours. On the other hand, in the neighbourhood of legitimate sharp changes in intensity (edges or lines), genuine detail will be blurred by averaging with pixels that should not be taken into the sum. The choice of window and its extent will have a profound effect on this blurring. This well illustrates a problem that pervades this level of processing - how do we distinguish between features that are genuine and those that should be removed? The property of being sharply different from neighbouring pixels is not enough, and it becomes necessary to look at the pattern of intensity within the window.

Three similar techniques, with different behaviour are;

(1)   Set

$$m(i,j) = \frac{1}{w} \sum_{(n,m) \in W} f(n,m)$$

the local average as before. Then, for some predetermined threshold T, set

$$g(i,j) = m(i,j) \qquad \text{if } |(f(i,j) - m(i,j))| > T$$

$$= f(i,j) \qquad \text{otherwise}$$

The effect of this modification is to prevent the change taking place unless it is considerable, where T determines what "considerable" means. We hope this will reduce blurring across genuine edges, but still rake out noise. It will still blur very sharp edges in areas where the window mean is considerably far away from the central pixel's grey level, though.

(2)   Instead of calculating the mean inside the window, we calculate the median *med* and set

$$g(i,j) = med$$

This scheme, called *median filtering*, requires at least a partial sort of the pixels in the window (which is clearly time consuming since it must be done at every position in the image) but many algorithms exist for doing this in an efficient manner (Huang et al., 1978).

(3)   Another refinement of the simple mean filter is *K-closest averaging* - some $K < w$ is chosen, the pixels in the window are ordered and the K pixels closest in intensity to the target pixel are averaged. The idea is to avoid bringing into the average pixels which are not in the same region as the target in the underlying image. This implies a heavier sorting load than just identifying the median.

These are just sample ideas; many algorithms of increasing complexity exist. Some are just elaborations of the simple ideas listed, and others will use these ideas in conjunction with an iterative scheme, hoping for a progressive refinement (Lev et al., 1976).

Feature Enhancement

It will frequently be the case that the features we wish to study are not highlighted; at least, not highlighted as much as they may be by suitable processing. A simple example of this is *background removal*; if we are lucky the background to an image (where "background" may be anything in which we are not principally interested) can be represented analytically, as $f_b(i,j)$ say. It is then a simple matter to form the image of interest;

$$g(i,j) = f(i,j) - f_b(i,j)$$

Common examples of such easily subtracted functions are a simple constant,

$$g(i,j) = f(i,j) - k \qquad \text{for some } k$$

or, perhaps in the presence of lighting to one side of the image, a simple linear function

$$g(i,j) = f(i,j) - (c_1 i + c_2 j + k) \qquad \text{for some } c_1, c_2, k$$

This idea is easily generalised to piecewise smooth backgrounds described by, for example, splines. If the feature of interest permits images to be captured "before and after" some event, then the pixel by pixel subtraction of the two will yield a good picture of what is changed; this is a technique sometimes used in medical applications where X-rays are taken before and after the administration of some radiographically visible treatment. The trick, of course, is the non-trivial one of matching the known ("before") features exactly in the "after" image in circumstances where the camera (or image acquisition apparatus) may have moved with respect to the "scene" between the captures.

Histograms

Another simple yet very widely used idea is *histogram manipulation*. It is easy to derive a histogram from an image by recording the number of pixels at particular grey levels; the histogram often yields useful information about the nature of the image. In Figure 4.2 for instance, the histogram shows that there is a bias toward the lower intensity grey levels; we could rightly deduce from this that a more equitable sharing of the pixels among the grey levels would affect the image appearance. This involves some transformation of the grey levels - what the transformation will be depends on the effect we wish to achieve, and can be deduced from the histogram.

Suppose that the image has (potentially) M grey levels (probably represented by intensities $0,1,2,...M-1$). We shall produce transformations $s=T(r)$, for $0 \leq r \leq M-1$, of these levels where it will be reasonable to assume that $0 \leq T(r) \leq M-1$ (so that we have the same grey level range) and that $T(r)$

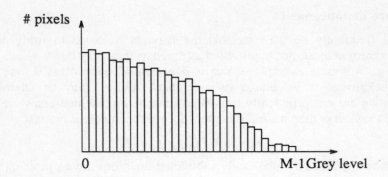

Figure 4.2 An intensity histogram

is monotonic (so that dark areas remain dark and light areas remain light). Such transformations just map grey levels so they do not alter the information in an image in the sense of the structure it may contain, but will enhance or suppress contrast, and stretch or compress grey level gradients.

An effective and simple example of this technique is *histogram equalisation* where the idea is to enhance use of "underused" grey levels and damp down use of "overused" ones. If the image is, say, N pixels square, we will be aiming for an image in which each grey level is occupied by N^2/M pixels (and is thus "equalised"). This is straightforward to achieve; writing *round* (x) for the closest integer to x, we set

$$n_r = \textit{number of pixels at grey level } r, \; 0 \le r \le M-1$$

and

$$t_r = \sum_{j=0}^{r} n_j = \textit{number of pixels at grey level } r \textit{ or less}$$

and then define

$$s = \mathbf{T}(r)$$

$$= \max(0, \textit{round}\,(\frac{Mt_r}{N^2}) - 1) \qquad\qquad 4.1$$

That is, determine how many pixels are at grey level r or less, calculate the closest multiple of N^2/M, subtract one and regard the result as the mapping s for r. Note this calculation ensures that $\mathbf{T}(0) \ge 0$, $\mathbf{T}(M-1) = M-1$ and $\mathbf{T}(r)$ is monotonic. The post-transformation image will not, generally, be precisely equalised; apart from effects due to the functions being digital we are at the mercy of very uneven input images. It is easy to see that if the input image has kN^2/M pixels at grey level 0, the output image of this transformation will not occupy grey levels $0...k-2$ at all since $T(0)=k-1$. The output should, however, have considerably enhanced contrast.

Table 4.1

Intensity r	n_r	$t_r = \sum\limits_{j=0}^{r} n_j$
0	3244	3244
1	3899	7143
2	4559	11702
3	2573	14275
4	1428	15703
5	530	16233
6	101	16334
7	50	16384

Example

The example is unrealistically small, but illustrates the algorithm. Suppose we have a 128 pixel square image, with the intensity at each pixel being between 0 and 7 inclusive, the intensities being distributed as in Table 4.1.

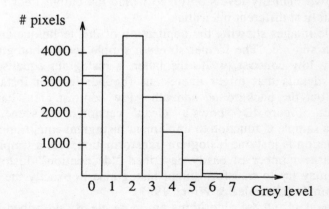

Figure 4.3 The input histogram

We see from the input histogram that the lower (darker) intensity levels predominate; an "equalised" histogram would have $N^2/M = 16384/8 = 2048$ grey levels at each intensity level.

pixels

Table 4.2

Intensity r	$\mathbf{T}(r) = round(\dfrac{t_r}{2048}) - 1$
0	1
1	2
2	5
3	6
4	7
5	7
6	7
7	7

Applying equation 4.1 defines the transformation shown in Table 4.2, and the transformed grey levels are distributed as in Table 4.3. Observe how the output histogram (Figure 4.4) is not equalised precisely (this would have been impossible without *selectively* transforming the input grey levels) but is considerably more "spread out" than the input. We cannot invent a spread that is not already potentially present; had the input image been binary (consisting of two intensity levels only), so would the output image have been, albeit possibly at different intensities.

Example images showing the application of this technique are shown in Figures 4.5 and 4.6. The former shows a simple scene photographed with deliberately low contrast, while the latter, a histogram equalised version, shows the details that might interest us (boundaries, for instance) much enhanced, but the background and other low contrast areas have become very mottled. Figure 4.16 shows a "clean" version of the scene. Appendix I contains a sample C function to implement histogram equalisation.

Equalisation is just one histogram transformation; it is a simple matter to define a large number of easily described "destination" histograms into which we may try to transform input histograms in exactly the same way. See for example (Gonzalez & Wintz, 1987).

Very frequently these algorithms are more clearly described by supposing that the grey levels are *continuous* in the interval $0 \leq r \leq 1$ and describing the transformations $\mathbf{T}(r)$ and $\mathbf{T}^{-1}(s)$ as continuous functions. It is a common trick in the study of discrete functions to apply results from the theory of continuous functions. If we take this approach, we can regard the histogram

Table 4.3

Intensity s	n_s	$t_s = \sum\limits_{j=0}^{s} n_j$
0	0	0
1	3244	3244
2	3899	7143
3	0	7143
4	0	7143
5	4559	11702
6	2573	14275
7	2109	16384

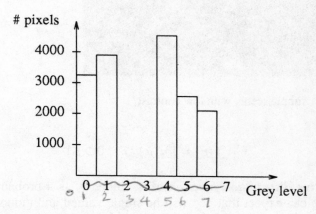

Figure 4.4 The output histogram

as a probability density function describing the distribution of the input grey levels r, $p_r(r)$. Now if $\mathbf{T}^{-1}$ satisfies the (likely) conditions of being monotonic increasing and single valued, elementary probability theory tells us (Fisz 1963)

$$p_s(s) = \left[p_r(r)\frac{dr}{ds} \right]_{r=\mathbf{T}^{-1}(s)} \qquad 4.2$$

To see what this means in the case of equalisation, consider the transformation

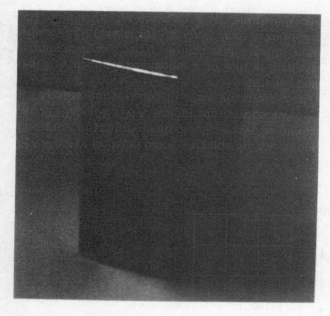

Figure 4.5 A simple scene, with low contrast

$$s = T(r) = \int_0^r p_r(u)\,du \qquad 0 \le r \le 1$$

the *cumulative distribution function* of r. Since p_r is a probability density function, we can expect that T^{-1} will be single valued and monotonic on the interval $[0,1]$; further, it is immediately clear that

$$\frac{ds}{dr} = p_r(r)$$

and hence

$$p_s(s) = \left[p_r(r) \frac{1}{p_r(r)} \right]_{r=T^{-1}(s)}$$

$$= [1]_{r=T^{-1}(s)}$$

$$= 1 \qquad 0 \le s \le 1$$

So $p_s(s)$ is identically 1 regardless of the nature of the function $\mathbf{T}^{-1}(s)$; such a density function corresponds to an equalised histogram, and we see the theory underlying the equalisation transformation derived in the discrete case.

Figure 4.6 An equalised version of Figure 4.5

This example is included only to illustrate a technique that is widespread in the formulation of these algorithms. The theory underpinning many of these ideas relies on continuous functions and it is only a final step to move the results into the discrete domain. The problem with the ideas just demonstrated lies in equation 4.2 above - an implied knowledge of the function $\mathbf{T}^{-1}(s)$. In our simple example this did not matter, but for less trivial "destination" density functions it will not, in general, be possible to derive $\mathbf{T}^{-1}$ analytically. This is where we are fortunate to be working in the discrete domain; if all else fails we can derive the inverse function numerically.

A good exposition of histogramming techniques and their underlying analysis can be found in (Gonzalez & Wintz, 1987).

Advanced Techniques

It is seen again and again in Image Processing that the simple algorithms are often the best; it is certainly true that their simplicity lends them to the most efficient implementation. Nevertheless, ideas such as histogram manipulation are, in the mathematical sense, never more than elementary; they never go far beyond attacking the most obvious features of an image. Beyond the simple ideas are a host of considerably more complicated algorithms relying on image *transforms*. It is a well known idea to transform functions into some "transform space" that exhibits features of the functions that we cannot normally access. These features may be processed in the transform space in some suitable way, and the result subjected to the inverse transform to acquire a manipulated version of the original function.

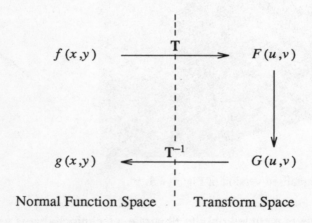

Figure 4.7 How transforms are used

Figure 4.7 shows this idea schematically; the function $f(x,y)$ is transformed to $F(u,v)$, and manipulated in some way. The resulting function $G(u,v)$ is subjected to the inverse transform to acquire $g(x,y)$ in "normal" function space; we may suppose that reaching g from f without recourse to the transform will be difficult or maybe impossible. The price to be paid here is that T and its inverse may prove to be very expensive computationally, and that the transformed functions F and G usually conceal many of the features we are accustomed to using, while highlighting the ones we do not normally see.

In Image Processing the best known transform by far is the two dimensional *Fourier Transform*. This book does not mean to teach Fourier theory (although see Appendix II for a brief exposition) but its definition is as follows; for a continuous function of two variables $f(x,y)$,

$$F(u,v) = \int\limits_{-\infty}^{\infty} \int\limits_{-\infty}^{\infty} f(x,y)\exp\left[-i\,2\pi(ux+vy)\right]dxdy \qquad 4.3$$

and the inverse is

$$f(x,y) = \int\limits_{-\infty}^{\infty} \int\limits_{-\infty}^{\infty} F(u,v)\exp\left[i\,2\pi(ux+vy)\right]dudv$$

Some worthwhile observations about the Fourier transform are

(1)   It is computationally very expensive; it involves repeated multiplications on floating point numbers and trigonometric calculations. A lot of work is done on deriving swift implementations of the transform, notably the *Fast Fourier Transform*, or FFT.

(2)   For general functions the integrals are difficult if not impossible to perform; our applications of the transform will be on discrete functions though, and performing both the transform and its inverse reduces to a (long) numerical computation.

(3)   The transform of f gives a measure of the *frequencies* present in f. The Fourier domain, in which the transformed functions $F(u,v)$ lie, is often called the *frequency domain* in contrast to the intensity image $f(x,y)$ which lies in the *spatial domain*. We could interpret the integral 4.3 as a limit sum of discrete harmonic terms, each one representing the contribution of a particular frequency. These ideas will not be explored here, but the purpose of the transform is to allow removal or enhancement of particular frequencies in the original image; high frequencies will be due to sharp changes (e.g. edges) and low frequencies will be due to areas of low contrast. One way then to enhance edges in an image is to take its Fourier transform, emphasise the high frequencies present and take the inverse transform of the result. What we get is an edge sharpened image at the cost of attenuating the low frequencies; visually, the resulting images look corrupt, but the feature of interest is highlighted. See Figure 4.8 for an example. This is a Fourier high-pass filter of the left image of Figure 4.16; here the low frequencies have been suppressed, thereby accentuating the high ones. The major edges are now sharper, and the outline of the writing on the box crisper, but the low contrast areas are attenuated.

(4)   We shall see shortly that convolutions are often natural operations to perform on images; they may be done by transforming the image, doing the convolution in the frequency domain, and then performing an inverse transform. As explained in Appendix II, function *convolution*, normally a very expensive operation, is relatively cheap to carry

Figure 4.8 A Fourier high filter of Figure 4.16

out in the Fourier domain since it reduces to pointwise function multiplication.

Many excellent references exist for Fourier theory (Gonzalez & Wintz, 1987, Pratt 1978); in addition, there are a number of other transforms that can be used in similar ways, of which the best known perhaps are the Walsh and Hadamard transforms. We shall not discuss them further here beyond noting that in practice there are are many elaborate libraries available to do all the work of performing transforms - the Spider library (Spider 1983) is one well known example. The nature of the transform also lends itself to special purpose (vector) architectures which in turn will have their own subroutine libraries.

Templating

Once we have a clean image exhibiting the features we regard as important, we can begin to locate and classify them. An elementary way of doing this, if the feature we are searching for is easily described as a "sub-image", is to take such a subimage and regard it as a *template* that we will hold at every possible position in the image, and ask where it "fits" best. For example, if we are looking for white triangles of a given size on a dark background, it is easy to digitise such a simple pattern (Figure 4.9 perhaps, where we assume that high grey levels represent "light") and look for similarities to it in the image.

0	0	0	0	0
0	0	64	0	0
0	127	255	127	0
127	255	255	255	127
0	0	0	0	0

Figure 4.9 A simple template

More formally, if the image is N pixels square and the template is W pixels square (so we assume $W < N$), we may have

Image grey levels: $f(\mathbf{w})$, $\mathbf{w} = (w_1, w_2)$, $1 \leq w_1, w_2 \leq N$

Template grey levels: $t(\mathbf{x})$, $\mathbf{x} = (x_1, x_2)$, $1 \leq x_1, x_2 \leq W$

(where we move to vector notation for convenience). We might then hold this template at all offsets in the image and define a measure of how close it is. A simple and obvious measure to choose would be the sum of square differences; thus we may evaluate

$$d^2(\mathbf{y}) = \sum_{\mathbf{x}} (f(\mathbf{x}+\mathbf{y}) - t(\mathbf{x}))^2$$

$$= \sum_{\mathbf{x}} (f^2(\mathbf{x}+\mathbf{y}) - 2f(\mathbf{x}+\mathbf{y})t(\mathbf{x}) + t^2(\mathbf{x}))$$

and determine the value of $\mathbf{y}$ that *minimises d^2*.

We see by inspection that $d^2(\mathbf{y}) \geq 0$, and is only equal to zero if the template matches the image exactly. Further, the quantity $t^2(\mathbf{x})$ is constant with respect to $\mathbf{y}$; if we also assume that $f^2(\mathbf{x}+\mathbf{y})$ varies slowly with respect to $\mathbf{y}$ (so we may regard it as "approximately constant") then the job of minimising d^2 becomes that of *maximising*

$$\sum_{\mathbf{x}} f(\mathbf{x}+\mathbf{y})t(\mathbf{x}) \qquad\qquad 4.4$$

- the *cross correlation* between f and t. The value of $\mathbf{y}$ maximising the

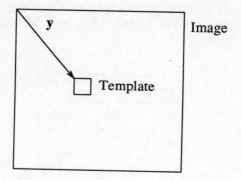

Figure 4.10 Find the "best fit"

expression 4.4 represents the "most likely" position of the template in the image.

Such simple correlation measures of template fit can and do work, but suffer serious drawbacks. Firstly, we see that each calculation of the correlation involves W^2 multiplications; since N is probably going to be an order of magnitude larger than W, there are going to be of the order of N^2 positions for the template, so the total number of multiplications involved will be of the order of W^2N^2 - this is a considerable amount of work.

In fact, what we are doing here amounts to *convolving* the template with the image, and is just the sort of job that is more efficiently done in the Fourier domain. For large templates especially, the image would probably be transformed first to allow the convolution to be done with maximum efficiency. This may be hard to believe since a "raw" Fourier transform of an $N \times N$ image costs of the order of N^4 multiplications (and so does its inverse), and the convolution in the Fourier domain will cost of the order of N^2 (see Appendix II). However, a variety of techniques exist to lessen the transform cost, in particular the Fast Fourier Transform mentioned above. One calculation (Niblack 1986) gives the following ratio in cost of real multiplications between the Fourier approach and a simple spatial domain convolution:

$$\frac{C_F(W,N)}{C_S(W,N)} = \frac{10N^2(\log_2 N)^2 + 2WN(\log_2 N) + 4N^2}{(N-W+1)^2 W^2}$$

where $C_F(W,N)$ is the cost of the Fourier convolution and $C_S(W,N)$ is the cost of the "spatial" convolution. Some sample values of these quantities for some W,N are given in Table 4.4.

Table 4.4

N	W	$C_S(W,N)$ $\times 10^6$	$C_F(W,N)$ $\times 10^6$
512	2	1.04	213.40
512	4	4.15	213.42
512	8	16.32	213.46
512	16	63.23	213.53
512	32	239.91	213.68

Theses "costs" refer only to the calculation of *one* convolution - if one image were to be subjected to several templates, or one template were to be offered up to several images, then the cost reduces appreciably since the transform only needs calculating once.

0	0	0	0	10	0	0	0	0
0	0	0	9	10	8	0	0	0
0	0	10	7	12	11	10	0	0
0	0	0	0	0	0	0	0	0
0	0	0	100	100	0	0	0	0
0	0	0	0	0	0	0	0	0

Figure 4.11 An image section

The simple templating idea also suffers from our assumption about the image. The approximation 4.4 is not valid if the image intensity varies significantly over areas the size of the template; further, surviving noise spikes will corrupt the measurement badly. Figure 4.11 illustrates how spurious information in the image can cause high correlation responses where there should be none - it shows a section of an image over which we will drag the template formed by deleting the top and bottom rows of Figure 4.9 (the zero rows). Figure 4.12 shows the correlation responses. The "correct" (or "best") position for the template is at the centre top of the image, but the maximum response is elsewhere, badly distorted by the noise spike at the bottom.

?	?	7002	12357	15539	12614	7895	?	?
?	?	3439	5155	5986	6111	3947	?	?
?	?	38840	51448	51768	38904	13340	?	?
?	?	12700	38200	38200	12700	0	?	?
?	?	?	?	?	?	?	?	?
?	?	?	?	?	?	?	?	?

Figure 4.12 Spurious correlation

Indeed it is usually unrealistic to search for whole objects in this fashion; it is unlikely to be successful if the orientation of the templated object is not known with certainty. A more promising idea is to use this technique to search for subparts of an object, in particular *edges*.

Edge Detection

Primitive edge detection is far less ambitious than template matching; it only tries to determine whether one edge (a component of a *boundary* in the image) passes through or near a given pixel. This is done by examining the rate of change of intensity near the pixel - sharp changes (steep gradients) are good evidence of an edge, slow changes will suggest the contrary. One of the simplest *edge operators* is due to Roberts (Roberts 1965) and involves offering up two templates to each pixel of the image; the two templates (see Figure 4.14) give a measure of intensity change in two orthogonal directions. For a pixel (i,j) the Roberts operator yields two numbers

$$\Delta_1 = f(i,j) - f(i+1,j+1)$$

Figure 4.13 An edge detection of Figure 1.1

$$\Delta_2 = f(i+1,j) - f(i,j+1)$$

We could then calculate the *gradient magnitude*

$$s(i,j) = \sqrt{\Delta_1^2 + \Delta_2^2}$$

or, less expensively,

$$s'(i,j) = |\Delta_1| + |\Delta_2|$$

to measure the rate of change of intensity near (i,j). Simply comparing s or s' with some suitably chosen threshold would then yield local edge information.

The Roberts edge operator is one of very many; it is common for them to take advantage of the underlying coordinate system and determine measures of the rate of change of intensity in the i and j directions. A very well known operator due to Sobel (Ballard & Brown, 1982) uses edge templates shown in Figure 4.15. We see at pixel (i,j) that the Sobel operator generates

$$\Delta_1 = (f(i+1,j-1)-f(i-1,j-1))+$$

$$2(f(i+1,j)-f(i-1,j))+$$

$$(f(i+1,j+1)-f(i-1,j+1))$$

$$\Delta_2 = (f(i-1,j+1)-f(i-1,j-1))+$$

$$2(f(i,j+1)-f(i,j-1))+$$

$$(f(i+1,j+1)-f(i+1,j-1))$$

The gradient magnitude may now be calculated in the same way as for the Roberts operator; we would hope that this operator would give a better result due to the local averaging implicit in the larger template. Note that it also allows an easy estimate of the *gradient direction* in the neighbourhood of pixel (i,j) as

$$\theta = \tan^{-1}(\frac{\Delta_2}{\Delta_1})$$

allowing us to see not only if an edge is present but also in which direction it is (probably) directed. Notice that the gradient direction is actually *normal* to the edge.

Figure 4.16 shows an example result of applying the Sobel edge operator. Here the threshold has been chosen to bring out the major features (the box edges) and it is clear to us what the picture depicts; notice though that the box edges are incomplete, and the "clutter" due to imperfectly defined features on one face of the box.

0	1
-1	0

1	0
0	-1

Figure 4.14 The Roberts edge operator templates

$i-1$ i $i+1$

-1	0	1	$j-1$	1	2	1
-2	0	2	j	0	0	0
-1	0	1	$j+1$	-1	-2	-1

inverted?

Figure 4.15 The Sobel edge templates

There are very many edge operators; some are similar to the ones shown here - simple first order gradient approximations (Prewitt 1970), or elaborations of similar ideas (Kirsch, 1971). Others pursue different strategies; we could, for example, have calculated second order differences, although this has the disadvantage of doubly enhancing the effects of noise. Figure 4.17 illustrates the principal of the *zero crossing* which is exploited in many modern edge detectors; at the top we have plotted grey levels along a line perpendicular to a boundary between a dark and a light region in an image. The intensity move from dark to light as we move along the line. Beneath, we look at the first derivative of this intensity function - the peak at the position of the edge is the feature that Sobel operators (for example) search for. The bottom graph shows the *second* derivative - the edge "position" coincides with the point at which this line crosses the horizontal axis - the "zero crossing".

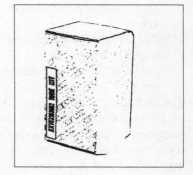

Figure 4.16 An image and its Sobel edge detection

The search for reliable edge detectors is an active area of research - Figure 4.13 shows the result of applying a more sophisticated edge detector to

Figure 1.1 (Wang 1987). It has done very well in finding the features of the scene, but notice that the glasses, cutlery and bottle are not at all well defined, and there are confusing lines on the plates (in passing, is there enough evidence to deduce the existence of a chair?). The detector due to Canny (Canny 1986) is widely used in modern Vision systems, while others (Jelinek & Mowforth, 1984) suggest that the whole approach of searching for elemental edges is wrong. Increasingly the effort is to produce algorithms suitable for post-processing by machines rather than human viewers. The operators described in this chapter were all developed as pure Image Processing tools; they suffer when there is noise in the image and can easily display false, or double, edges. This latter problem occurs in regions of sharp intensity changes stretching over more than a couple of pixels - primitive edge detectors may register this as parallel edges where there should only be one; this problem is exacerbated if the underlying image has been subjected to some filter that induces blur as a side effect. Further, these filters demand a choice of threshold, usually by human intervention when we would have preferred the whole process to be automatic. The ideal operator will have rather more intelligence about global features of the image than these very local templates can ever acquire.

Exercises

(1) Write a program that implements K-closest averaging. As far as you can, analyse its complexity and suggest how it may be speeded up.

(2) Write a program that, given an image array, introduces noise
  (i) Uniformly distributed in the range $[-n, +n]$ for an input parameter n.
  (ii) Normally distributed with mean 0 and standard deviation an input parameter σ.
  (iii) Uniformly distributed in the range $[0, +n]$ for an input parameter n.

  [In each case, the intensity of a corrupted pixel should be constrained to lie in the same range as those of the uncorrupted image]. Run the program on some sample images and plot the results.
  Describe an algorithm that may be used to remove noise of type *(iii)*.

(3) Implement and run the histogram equaliser listed in Appendix I.

(4) Transform the example in the text so that its histogram approximates to the following probability density functions;
  (i) $p(x) = \frac{1}{2} + x$ $0 \leq x \leq 1$
  (ii) $p(x) = \frac{3}{4} + x$ $0 \leq x \leq \frac{1}{2}$

$$p(x) = \frac{7}{4} - x \qquad \qquad \tfrac{1}{2} \leq x \leq 1$$

What do these transformations achieve?

(5) Appendix I includes a C function that implements a Sobel edge operator. Amend this function to return edge magnitude and direction, and run it on some sample images.

(6) Suggest a possible set of 5x5 edge templates.

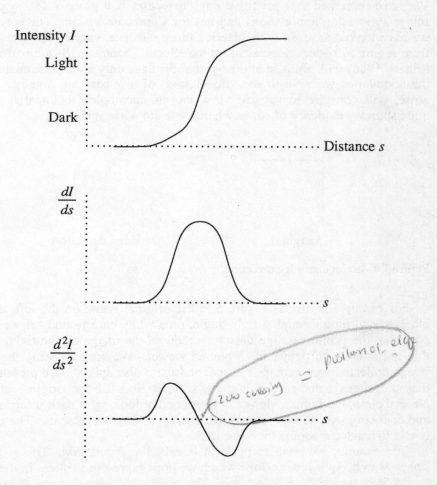

Figure 4.17 An edge profile, and its derivatives

CHAPTER 5

Segmentation

We have remarked that primitive edge detection is a process designed for Image Processing applications and not for Computer Vision. The schemes we have looked at, even with adaptive thresholds (i.e. varying the threshold from region to region, dependent on the ''local'' contrast) (Swaminathan & Srihari, 1986) will result in an image that displays only an approximation to the boundaries we wish to see. Local areas of low contrast, together with noise, will conspire to suggest very uneven, incomplete boundaries with quite spurious evidence of edges where there are noise spikes.

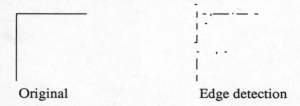

Original   Edge detection

Figure 5.1 Inadequate edge detection

For example, consider Figure 5.1; the original scene on the left was a black line turning through a right-angle, on a white background - if we suppose that the primitive edge detector produces the image on the right, then that is probably sufficient for a human viewer. We are supposing that the image collected was perhaps blurred, and that noise spikes were present, so that the edges detected are not the straight lines of the original at all. Nevertheless, the human viewer is very good at looking at such information and deducing with some accuracy what it ''probably'' represents. The problem is to teach a machine the same trick.

The exercise we wish to perform is called *segmentation*. The original image is to be split into *regions* which we hope represent *surfaces* in the real world from which the image came. The purpose of segmentation is to pass onto subsequent algorithms a symbolic representation of the scene rather than the pixel grid at which we have been looking so far. Ideally we want to be able to say something like ''The scene consists of a circle, radius r, centred at (a,b) intersecting a square, side s, centred at (x,y)'', although such a complete and formulaic description is unlikely except in exceptionally simple applications - at the very least, we want the segmentation phase to dispense with the pixel-based information and to parameterise the scene in a more concise and meaningful way. This does not yet necessarily imply an extraction of three dimensional information.

Segmentation then has two purposes. The first is to make some identifications in the image; in a car park scene, perhaps, the object would be to locate cars and dispense with all other information. Secondly we want a compaction of the data; if we can take as input an image of ASCII text and extract from it the occurrence and order of the characters, then each letter's representation will have been reduced from perhaps hundreds of pixels to just seven bits. This phase of a Vision system would be an intermediate step that would pass its findings on for post processing by a higher level stage.

Segmentation by Histogram

Many scenes, in industrial applications for instance, consist simply of an object on a uniform background, or perhaps a slowly varying background. Such a scene is very straightforward to segment simply by looking at its histogram; we shall expect the histogram to have two peaks, one corresponding to the background and one to the object, similar to Figure 5.2.

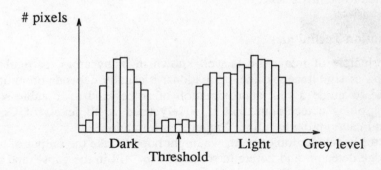

Figure 5.2 A Bimodal histogram

Note we are not saying that the intensity is the same throughout the region occupied by the object or the background, merely that they are distinguishable from each other, so the peaks of the histogram need not be sharp - all we require is that the trough be easy to detect. Quite probably there will be edges and regions within the object - all this technique will perform is a "large scale" segmentation to locate the object. The idea is simple; any pixel whose intensity is less than the threshold at the histogram trough is deemed to lie in one region, and those above are deemed to lie in the other region. (An example is shown in Chapter 6). Such a scheme will not produce clearly defined, straight boundaries, but should give us a good first approximation which may be quite enough for an unambiguous recognition of the scene.

It is quite possible that the background, while locally constant or near constant, varies over the extent of the image to such a degree that no threshold is suitable; if this occurs, then the histogram peak corresponding to the background is wide and low, as opposed to narrow and high, and probably overlapping with the peak due to the object so much as to make them indistinguishable. We can still use the simple thresholding idea by dividing the image into (probably rectangular) sub-images; if the sub-images are small enough, we can hope that the bimodal feature of the histogram reappears since the sub-image is small enough to make the contrast quite clear again. Then a threshold is chosen, appropriate to each sub-image; those that do not exhibit bimodal histograms should have thresholds interpolated from their neighbours. This scheme has been very successfully used (Chow & Kaneko, 1972) to detect ventricles in cardioangiograms.

Figure 6.1 in the next Chapter shows an image segmentation performed by this technique. While this may seem a very simple idea, it will have live applications in many industrial situations where lighting conditions may be expected to be favourable.

Relaxation Techniques

The principle of relaxation is well known in many areas, particularly the solution of simultaneous linear equations; it usually depends on an iterative scheme to guide a first approximation of some kind to a stable solution. Relaxation is a technique that is widely used at all levels of Computer Vision in attempting to refine ''impure'' information.

In the segmentation context, we might hope to take the output of a primitive edge detector, and iterate in some way to ''fill in the gaps'' and remove the effects of noise. We would hope to do this on the basis of edge information in the neighbourhood of a particular pixel; if, as in Figure 5.3, there is strong evidence for edges in pixels either side of another pixel, we may deduce that we should insert an edge to produce a continuous boundary. Better, we should attach *probabilities* to the existence of edges at all possible points, and increment the probability of an edge in such a position. Likewise, edges which appear ''isolated'' in their particular neighbourhood should have their probabilities reduced. These ideas can be applied to an image in several passes, hoping to reach a stable state where true edges have probability 1, and all others have had their probabilities reduced to 0. This would leave us with continuous boundaries reflecting the regions in the original image.

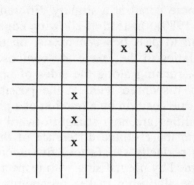

Figure 5.3 Scope for iteration

The algorithm may be implemented in several ways; at its simplest (Schafter et al., 1977) a primitive edge operator is passed over the image and used to generate edge probabilities (by, for example, taking the ratio of the gradient magnitude to the maximum gradient magnitude in the image) and first approximations to gradient direction for each pixel. These are then iteratively influenced by the pixels in an immediate neighbourhood to update the probabilities and directions - neighbouring pixels that have edge evidence in similar directions will enhance probabilities while "contradictory" edges will damp them.

A refinement of the idea (Zucker et al., 1977) is to quantise the gradient directions into eight equally spaced angles in the range $(-\pi/2, \pi/2]$, together with a ninth "null" direction to denote no edge, and a probability is assigned to each of these nine at each pixel, again derived initially from some primitive edge operator. The relaxation scheme then iterates each of these nine probabilities at each pixel using evidence of "smoothness" of gradient to enhance probabilities and evidence of gradient contradictions to damp them. Characteristically, some convergence is seen in less than a dozen iterations of such schemes.

There are many potential elaborations to these ideas; the drawback is the level of complexity that develops in algorithms that are pursuing an essentially simple idea. In the scheme just described, we need to construct an array of "compatibility coefficients" to describe the likely interaction of edges of the nine possible types and their directions. This array can only be derived by heuristic means, and is likely to run into difficulties at boundary junctions, where three or more legitimate edges are present. In any event, tuning the algorithm will be a subtle business, with no clear proof that it will be running optimally.

We now look in more detail at a slightly different idea that makes life much simpler (Prager 1980). Instead of allowing edges to pass through pixels, we constrain them to pass *between* pixels, on the *crack edges* - this implies that all boundaries in the image are composed of short horizontal and vertical segments, running along the sides of pixels. The problem of edge direction is now dispensed with, at the possible cost of displacing boundaries from their true position by a fraction of a pixel.

The initial probabilities are now straightforward to calculate; for each "crack edge" we form the absolute difference of the intensities to either side, a very crude but perfectly satisfactory first approximation. Probabilities would now be formed by normalising with respect to the maximum such difference, C say. The algorithm makes no attempt to inhibit boundaries from performing right angle turns, so we see that *a priori*, each elemental edge has six possible neighbours (see Figure 5.4). In this figure, we suppose that the neighbouring edges are labelled with their "probabilities", a_i, b_i.

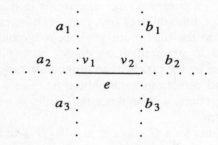

Figure 5.4 The neighbours of a crack edge

We now associate an integer between 0 and 3 inclusive with each end of the edge according to the "likely" number of boundaries in the image that are coincident at that point. Consider the left hand end of the edge $e(v_1,v_2)$ in Figure 5.4 and assume, without loss of generality, that $a_1 \geq a_2 \geq a_3$. A simple probabilistic argument tells us that, neglecting for the moment whether or not $e(v_1,v_2)$ itself is a true edge in the image,

$$Pr(No\ coincident\ edges) = (1-a_1)(1-a_2)(1-a_3) \qquad 5.1$$

$$Pr\,(Exactly\ 1\ edge) = a_1(1-a_2)(1-a_3) \qquad\qquad 5.2$$

$$Pr\,(Exactly\ 2\ edges) = a_1a_2(1-a_3) \qquad\qquad 5.3$$

$$Pr\,(Exactly\ 3\ edges) = a_1a_2a_3 \qquad\qquad 5.4$$

Taking the maximum of these four gives the number of edges m likely to be coincident at the left hand end; a similar calculation on the b_i provides the number n at the right hand end. The resulting (unordered) integer pair (m,n) is used as the basis of the relaxation.

Some incremental probability value is chosen at the outset; values in the range 0.05 to 0.20 have been found to be successful. During an iteration of the algorithm an edge's probability is *increased* by this amount if (m,n) is one of

$$(1,1) \quad (1,2) \quad (1,3)$$

and *decreased* by this amount if (m,n) is one of

$$(0,0) \quad (0,2) \quad (0,3)$$

in both cases the adjustment being done subject to the constraint that the resulting probability lies in the range 0 to 1. Other (m,n) pairs result in no adjustment.

The reasoning here is that, in the former case, there is evidence of a "loose" edge that needs connecting to something else for whose existence there is also evidence; in the latter case there is no evidence that e would be connecting two boundary segments. For example, in Figure 5.5 e has three strong edges at one end and one at the other, so is of type (1,3); it seems likely that e does appear as an edge in the image, connecting a boundary "end" to create an intersection of four boundary segments. We would thus enhance the probability associated with e. The difficulty with this algorithm is edges of type (0,1) where one end appears to be a "loose end" of some kind, while the other appears to be in space; if we elect to enhance the probability of such an edge we may just be propagating noise. If on the other hand we damp it, we may be inhibiting a genuine boundary. The problem cannot be resolved without looking further afield, and therefore it is just left alone.

In practice, equations 5.1 - 5.4 are not suitable; in the event of a_1 being considerably larger than a_2 and a_3, but still less than 0.5, the probability of no edges predominates, but we would want an indication of one edge at the left of e rather than none. We can achieve this by looking at the probabilities with respect to their local maximum, and rewriting the equations as;

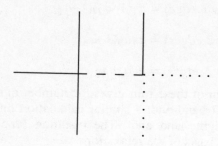

Figure 5.5 An example (1,3) edge

$$m = \max(a_1, a_2, a_3, q)$$

$$Pr\,(No\ coincident\ edges) = (m-a_1)(m-a_2)(m-a_3)$$

$$Pr\,(Exactly\ 1\ edge) = a_1(m-a_2)(m-a_3)$$

$$Pr\,(Exactly\ 2\ edges) = a_1 a_2(m-a_3)$$

$$Pr\,(Exactly\ 3\ edges) = a_1 a_2 a_3$$

The threshold q is introduced to prevent the probability of no edges always equating to zero; experimental evidence suggests that values around 0.1 to 0.3 for q are suitable.

[In fact, an implementation of this algorithm would avoid any of the expensive floating point arithmetic implied by these probability manipulations. Everything that has been described can be scaled up and performed in integers with respect to the maximum crack edge difference C].

Figure 5.6 shows two iterations from an application of this algorithm to Figure 1.1, one rather earlier than the other. Notice how features such as a plate, the third glass and the tablecloth edge are much more visible in the second picture; the further noise we have incurred could be raked out by post-processing. This algorithm usually seems to give good "convergence" after about five iterations; further, it lends itself to useful post-processing. The iteration encourages the formation of boundaries around regions; after it is complete we can quickly determine which vertices represent boundary junctions or end points as those where 1, 3 or 4 edges are incident. Thus we can locate boundary segments that separate only two regions - in practice we would accumulate a list of these segments and determine properties of them such as

endpoint coordinates

length in "crack edges"

Euclidean length

mean and variance intensity contrast across the boundary

mean and variance of intensities on either side of the boundary.

These properties are a good springboard for determining properties of the bounded region, such as "straightness" of its boundaries, and homogeneity of intensity. It will also allow the detection of unlikely boundaries such as those that are short or across which there is a large variance in contrast. These post-processing steps are described in more detail in the original reference (Prager 1980).

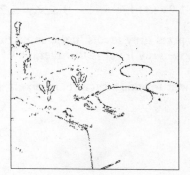 

Figure 5.6 Two iterations of a relaxation algorithm

The common feature of relaxation algorithms in the context of segmentation is that they are essentially heuristic - there is no good theory to back them up as there is for relaxation applications in the solution of, for example, simultaneous equations. The number of iterations required and the thresholds and increments necessary need to be determined by experiment, and there is no guarantee of convergence. That said, the techniques are very successful, particularly for geometrically irregular scenes that are not easily parameterised, such as outdoor scenes.

Hierarchical Techniques

Most of the work load in passing edge detectors over images is due to the sheer number of pixels at which they have to look. Much of this work is wasted - the human viewer can see very quickly which areas of an image are region interiors and which are likely to contain boundaries - armed with this "coarse" information the brain then seems to apply higher resolution to specific areas of interest to separate regions with more precision. *Hierarchical* techniques mimic this behaviour by sacrificing resolution at early stages in order to form approximate ideas about where boundaries lie.

If we suppose that we have a square image I whose side length N is a power of 2, $N = 2^n$ then we can define images recursively $I_n, I_{n-1}, ..., I_0$ as follows;

$$I_n = I$$

$$I_{i-1}(x,y) = \frac{1}{4}[\, I_i(2x,2y) + I_i(2x+1,2y) +$$

$$I_i(2x,2y+1) + I_i(2x+1,2y+1)\,] \qquad 0 \le x,y \le 2^{i-1}$$

so, for $0 \le i \le n$, I_i is a 2^i by 2^i image with pixel grey levels in the same range as I; in particular, I_0 is a single pixel whose grey level is the average of the intensities in I.

Observe that the total storage requirement for this structure, in pixels, is

$$\sum_{i=0}^{n} 2^i 2^i = \sum_{i=0}^{n} 2^{2i}$$

$$= \frac{4.2^{2n} - 1}{3}$$

$$\approx (\frac{4}{3}). \ number \ of \ pixels \ in \ I$$

so despite generating a lot of images, the storage load is not prohibitive compared to that required for I alone.

The intermediate images will suffer increasing amounts of blurring as their resolution is reduced. While detail may be lost, this will not matter if we are only looking for the major features, or at least the approximate nature of the major features. Figure 5.7 shows a sequence of images that have been condensed thus; these are the three images immediately "above" that shown on the left of Figure 4.16 (so the smallest has a side length in pixels one sixteenth of the original). Note the blurring and declining level of detail, but the retention of major features. Such a sequence is often referred to as a *pyramid* of images, the apex of the pyramid being I_0 and the base I_n.

The fact that major regions are distinguishable at lower resolution can be exploited by the following segmentation algorithm (Tanimoto & Pavlidis, 1975). We choose the highest level of the pyramid (that is, the lowest value of i) at which the features we wish to detect are retained in I_i, and pass a primitive edge operator across it. At every pixel at which this operator gives

Figure 5.7 An image pyramid

evidence for an edge greater than some threshold, we descend the pyramid one layer and pass the edge detector over the four pixels that were used to form it. This process is performed recursively until $I_n=I$ is reached, at which point we have performed the edge detection on the original image. The edge operator is not applied at any point of I except those reached by these means.

This idea has two main advantages over simply applying edge operators to the original image; firstly the averaging process of going up the pyramid has the effect of distinguishing the major regions with respect to background and each other, albeit at the cost of blurring their edges. This it does by clearing the effects of noise which is lost in the averaging - as a result, the edge operator is rarely applied to the pixels at which noise is present and spurious regions are lost from the segmentation. Secondly, it is conspicuously cheaper in computation terms; characteristically this algorithm will be started about a third of the way up the pyramid at an image with about $2^{4n/3}$ pixels instead of 2^{2n}, and the edge operator will only be applied at lower levels where strictly necessary. Since it is the application of the operator that represents the cost in time, we can see that this algorithm will run much faster than applying operators to each pixel of the image I.

Appendix I includes a sample C function that implements a hierarchical (pyramidal) edge detector.

Hough Transforms

We have only looked so far at ideas that will define where the regions in an image are and have done nothing about interpreting what they may be. It will obviously be important to know if, for example, a region is circular, or if a boundary segment is a straight line. This is the sort of information that is not immediately available - in particular we are at the mercy of the digitisation, so that circles will not be defined by perfect arcs, and straight lines that are not strictly horizontal or vertical will exhibit "staircase" behaviour. Further, if a simple feature is incomplete, perhaps because it is occluded, we still want to be told that it is there.

For example, in Figure 5.8 we want to be told that (probably) there is a square partially occluding a circle which in turn partially occludes another square, together with the dimensions, location and orientation of the figures. A list of boundary segments is not on its own going to provide this information - the *Hough Transform* (Hough 1962) aims to bypass the detection of boundaries and generate information about parameterised features such as circles and straight lines direct from information about edge locations.

As its name suggests, the Hough transform does its work in a transform or *parameter* space; the parameters in question are those used to describe the

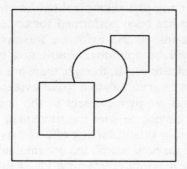

Figure 5.8 Square occludes circle occludes square

feature for which we are looking. As an example of the technique, we suppose that we wish to locate circles of radius R in an image. Such a circle centred at (a,b) has equation

$$(x-a)^2+(y-b)^2 = R^2$$

in Cartesian coordinates, or parametrically

$$(a+R\cos\theta, b+R\sin\theta) \quad 0\leq\theta<2\pi \qquad\qquad 5.5$$

Suppose we have knowledge that there is an edge at pixel (x,y): this knowledge would probably be generated by an edge operator. The edge may be part of a circle, or part of another feature, or just noise; if though it *is* part of one of the circles for which we are searching then we know that the centre of this circle must satisfy

$$(a,b) = (x+R\cos\theta, y+R\sin\theta) \quad 0\leq\theta<2\pi$$

that is it must lie on a circle of radius R centred at (x,y). This equation is a "dual" of equation 5.5, and a similar one can be generated for every pixel in the image at which we think there is an edge.

We now define a *parameter space* in which the parameters of the circle for which we are searching, a and b, reside. This parameter space will (probably) be quantised in the same manner as the original image, except that we may permit the circle centre to lie outside the image. If we wanted to restrict the location of the circle though, this is the opportunity to do it by restricting the range(s) of a, b as necessary. Now in this parameter space we define an *accumulator array* $A[a,b]$, initially erased to zeroes, for all possible values of a and b. For each (x,y) that we suppose is an edge, we now increment all members of the accumulator array $A[a,b]$ for which (a,b) is a solution of equation 5.5. By these means we are collecting all appropriate evidence for any particular pixel to be a circle centre.

When this operation has been performed for each likely edge pixel, the accumulator array contains all the evidence for circles from all over the image; some of this will be spurious, contributed by noise or legitimate edges that are not part of circles. If, though, there are circles of radius R, we will expect their centres to accumulate a lot of evidence - for each point on their boundary there will be an increment to the accumulator array at the centre, or near it. We cannot be sure the increment will occur at the true centre since quantisation or other blurring effects may displace it by a pixel or two. For this reason we now search the accumulator array for *local maxima*; particularly strong maxima represent a lot of evidence for circles. In Figure 5.9 for example, we would deduce evidence for a circle at centre (r,s). Figure 6.3 in the next Chapter illustrates this by representing the accumulator array as an intensity image.

	r			
42	31	233	23	40
43	54	280	51	38
34	52	282	67	30
31	48	232	96	29
30	41	146	90	23

(with s labelling the rows)

Figure 5.9 Local maxima in the array

The interesting thing about this algorithm is that it is very good at recognising *partial* circles since it does not need the circumference points from which it generates evidence to be consecutive or complete; the partial evidence available is sufficient to distinguish the centre from spurious evidence in the accumulator array. There are many techniques for locating circles in images (Illingworth & Kittler, 1985) but this one has been determined to be the most accurate, and the only one that can generate reliable evidence from partial features. The drawback is the computational load it introduces; determining all possible solutions to equation 5.5 for all possible edge pixels will be very time consuming. This becomes far more of a problem when we do not know the circle radius in advance. It should be clear that we can extend parameter space to three dimensions (R,a,b) and regard the circle radius as variable too. This will involve incrementing a three dimensional parameter array for all plausible centres of all edge pixels (that is, all (R,a,b) satisfying 5.5 for a given edge pixel (x,y)), but the cost is now very substantial.

One way of cutting down the work load (Kimme et al., 1975) is to make use of the gradient direction at each putative edge pixel. In the algorithm as described, we permitted the possibility of a circle centre in any direction from the edge provided it was at distance R. If, though, the gradient direction is known then this tells us the direction in which the circle centre must lie, and cuts a considerable amount of work out of the algorithm.

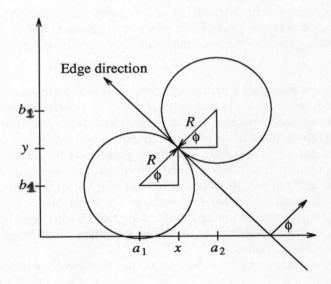

Figure 5.10 Edge direction and circle centres

More specifically, if we know there is a likely edge at pixel (x,y) and that the direction of that edge is ϕ, then if this edge lies on a circle of radius R, elementary geometry, illustrated in Figure 5.10, shows that the circle is centred at either (a_1,b_1) or (a_2,b_2) where

$$a_1 = x - R\cos\phi \quad b_1 = y - R\sin\phi$$

and

$$a_2 = x + R\cos\phi \quad b_2 = y + R\sin\phi$$

In fact, we will not be certain that the direction is correct; if we suppose that the maximum error we incur in the calculation of the direction is δφ (where δφ=π/4 might be a reasonable choice) then we increment all points in the accumulator array $A[a,b]$ (or $A[R,a,b]$ if the radius is unknown) that are solutions of

$$a = x + R\cos\theta \quad b = y + R\sin\theta$$

where

$$\phi - \delta\phi \le \theta \le \phi + \delta\phi \quad \text{or} \quad -\phi - \delta\phi \le \theta \le -\phi + \delta\phi \qquad 5.6$$

Experiments show that this technique is much swifter than the crude approach and also very reliable.

The Hough transform generalises well to easily parameterised curves - in particular conic sections lend themselves to an approach very similar to that used for hunting circles. As a second example, consider straight lines

$$\boxed{y = mx + c} \qquad 5.7$$

We can construct an (m,c) parameter space, and increment an array $A[m,c]$ for all values of m and c satisfying 5.7 for a particular likely edge pixel (x,y); then the local maxima in the accumulator array will tell us which pairs (m,c) represent lines on which many points lie, and in fact the value in the accumulator tells us exactly how many points. There are two problems with this approach; firstly the quantisation of (m,c) space is difficult since not only are arbitrarily high values of m possible, but their admission to the calculation is desirable ($m=\infty$ representing a vertical line). Secondly if a straight line appears in an image it will be signaled by the algorithm even if it is partial, so does not extend to the image boundary - the Hough algorithm cannot tell us its end points.

The first problem may be solved by noting that the equation 5.7 may be rewritten

$$r = x\cos\theta + y\sin\theta \qquad 5.8$$

where

$$\theta = \tan^{-1}(-\frac{1}{m}) \quad r = c\sin\theta$$

(see Figure 5.11). Now m lying in the range $(-\infty,\infty)$ is represented by θ lying in the *finite* range $[0,\pi]$; we can quantise (r,θ) space in the normal way and solve 5.8 for appropriate r and θ at each edge (x,y).

An application of this algorithm is shown in Figure 5.12, where we have search Figure 5.15 for straight lines. Notice that the endpoints of the lines are not indicated, while one of the cube edges which should be vertical has

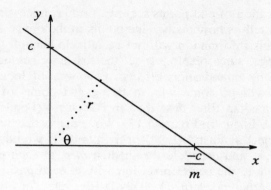

Figure 5.11 Rewriting $y = mx + c$

been detected as just "off vertical". Further, not all the cube edges have been found - because the Hough algorithm was using an inadequate edge detector as the source of its evidence, there was insufficient information in the original image to locate them.

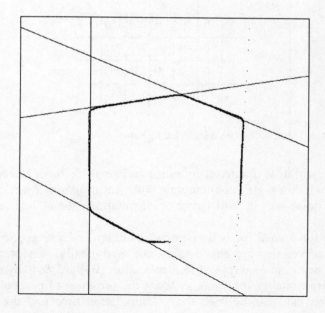

Figure 5.12 The straight lines of Figure 5.15

The identification of end points requires further processing; the accumulator array does tell us how many edge points in the image actually lie on a given line but this information will not be reliable enough for us to delimit lines in the image, since pixels just off the line may belong to it and have been displaced by quantisation effects. One way of locating corners of regions, which will go some way to fixing end points of lines, is a by-product of the median filter described in Chapter 4 (Foglein et al., 1984). Consider the sub-image in Figure 5.13. We suppose that we see the (dark) corner of an object against a (light) background. If we now pass a 3 by 3 window over this, and calculate the median *med* at each position, we see that *med* is equal to the centre pixel intensity at each position except when centred at the corner pixel (p, q). This is illustrated in Figure 5.14. This suggests the following algorithm; pass a median filter over the image and calculate the difference in magnitude of the median and centre pixels. If this difference exceeds some threshold, regard the pixel as a likely corner.

p

	255	255	255	255	255
	255	255	255	255	255
q	0	0	0	255	255
	0	0	0	255	255
	0	0	0	255	255

Figure 5.13 A black corner on a light background

This algorithm is disturbed by noise and small features (features thinner than the window); in conjunction with information from the Hough transform however, it will permit information about line ends to be extracted.

The Hough transform is a powerful technique whose application is not limited to curves that are easy to describe analytically. Chapter 6 includes Figures showing an example of its application (Ballard & Brown, 1982). It generates high quality information about the presence of particular features, but the price paid can be high too. Computation time and the size of the accumulator array increase exponentially as the number of parameters goes up, and only the very simplest features can be described with small numbers of parameters. Nevertheless, the value and power of the technique have encouraged researchers to develop fast (more efficient) uses of the transform (Illingworth & Kittler, 1987) in order that it can be exploited without suffering undue cost.

	p				
?	?	?	?	?	
?	255	255	255	?	
?	0	255	255	?	
?	0	0	255	?	
?	?	?	?	?	

Figure 5.14 A median filter pass over Figure 5.13

Region Growing Techniques

Another way of approaching the segmentation problem is logically the "dual" of boundary detection; regions are isolated not by determining their boundaries but by their interiors. Such duplicate ideas should, of course, lead to exactly the same result as a boundary detected segmentation, but their availability permits a degree of versatility in deciding how best to segment an image. The assumption will be that, whatever the regions in an image represent, their is some feature of them that can be exploited to distinguish them from each other. At the level at which we are working this will probably be grey level related; in very clean, simple images it may be enough just to segment pixels into groups having the same or very close grey levels (this is essentially what the histogram technique mentioned earlier did) but in general, grey levels will vary across a region and diffuse lighting will not always allow boundaries to display the level of contrast for which we might hope. Figure 5.15 shows an image that displays these features of "vagueness" that the human eye can resolve easily but that machines find difficult - this picture was taken with deliberately low contrast to illustrate how hard it can be to detect the "internal" edges.

One approach is to make a very crude, unintelligent segmentation which is known to be too simple, perhaps just by marking groups of pixels of the

Figure 5.15 A low contrast picture of a cube

same intensity as regions. Such a segmentation will have far too many regions, and we shall try selectively to *merge* them into fewer, larger regions, hoping to iterate towards a "correct" segmentation. One such scheme (Brice & Fennema, 1970) uses the "crack edges" of the relaxation algorithm examined earlier. The description presented here follows the original reference quite closely.

Suppose that a crude region detector has been passed over the image that places all pixels *within* regions, so that boundaries run along the crack edges. We look at pixels x, y on either side of a particular edge that is part of a boundary, and define

$$s(x,y) = |f(x) - f(y)|$$

the difference in intensity level across the edge to be the crack edge *strength* for that particular edge. If the image has M grey levels, this strength will be in the range $0,...,M-1$. Then, for some threshold T_1, $0 \leq T_1 \leq M-1$, define the *weakness* of the edge as

$$w(x,y) = 1 \qquad if \; s(x,y) < T_1$$

$$= 0 \qquad otherwise$$

The strategy will be to look at weakness along a whole boundary segment rather than just locally to any particular edge. Consider Figure 5.16; we suppose that the regions R_1, R_2 have perimeters (measured in crack edges) P_1, P_2 respectively, and that their common boundary (also measured in crack edges) is B. We can define the *weakness* of B in the obvious way as

$$w(B) = \sum_B w(\mathbf{x,y})$$

the sum of the weaknesses of the elemental edges.

There are now two heuristics we can pass over the image. The *phagocyte heuristic* chooses a threshold T_2, $0 \le T_2 \le 1$, and merges R_1 and R_2 if

$$\frac{w(B)}{\min(P_1,P_2)} > T_2$$

while the *weakness heuristic* chooses a threshold T_3, $0 \le T_3 \le 1$, and merges R_1 and R_2 if

$$\frac{w(B)}{B} > T_3$$

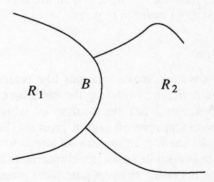

Figure 5.16 Two regions joined by B

The weakness heuristic looks rather more natural; it simply compares the weakness of the boundary segment with its length. In practice, however, it is found that using this alone produces an over enthusiastic merging and many true boundaries are lost. The problem is solved by repeatedly passing the phagocyte heuristic over the image *first* until it merges no more regions; it is more selective since it depends on the whole region perimeters, and produces a much less crude segmentation to which the weakness heuristic can successfully be applied.

Suppose that R_1 and R_2 are merged by the phagocyte heuristic; we shall call the resulting region R and its perimeter P_R. If we assume $P_1 \geq P_2$ then

$$P_R = P_1 + P_2 - 2B$$

and

$$B \geq w(B) \geq P_2 T_2$$

so

$$P_R < P_1 + \frac{B}{T_2} - 2B$$

$$= P_1 + B\left(\frac{1}{T_2} - 2\right)$$

This equation gives us an idea of the effect on boundary perimeter of the choice of T_2. In particular, if $T_2 > \frac{1}{2}$, the boundary must shrink while if $T_2 < \frac{1}{2}$ it may grow.

Following these heuristics we would hope to have an accurate crack edge segmentation. It would require another pass over the image to convert the boundary segments to plausible straight line or arc segments connecting vertices at the meeting of three or more regions.

A Semantic Extension

There are many ways we can make schemes like region growing more elaborate (Zucker 1976), perhaps by refining the merging criteria or introducing new criteria, but no account has been taken of what the image actually *represents*. One way to improve on region growers (Feldman & Yakimovsky, 1974) and to make the algorithm less *ad hoc* is to introduce *semantics*, in the sense that the regions will be assigned interpretations in the context of what the scene represents rather than on pure local intensity information; we shall do this on a probabilistic basis.

Firstly consider the problem of assigning "meaning" to some putative segmentation, derived perhaps from one of the schemes described above. We assume that the scene comes from some "well known" category with classifiable regions; for example if we were looking at a picture of a dinner table, the regions would be *table, dinner plate, side plate, glass, ...* This *domain dependent* knowledge will be used to classify regions according to measurable properties. Obvious properties will be region size and perimeter (both absolute and relative), mean intensity, variation in intensity and shape; for example, a dinner plate will probably be elliptical and be larger than a piece of cutlery; further, intensity of a plate region may have low variance, but intensity variance over a table may be expected to be higher due to, say, shadows or pattern effects.

None of these features is certain; sometimes plates will have, or will appear to have, straight boundaries; sometimes the reflections on cutlery or glass will cause them to be near unrecognizable (see Figures 1.1 and 4.13). All we can do is assign *probabilities* that a region has a particular interpretation based on the features we elect to measure - for the algorithm to be described these probabilities would be determined in an initial *learning* phase during which a number of correct segmentations and interpretations would be classified. This results in a *classification tree*; the tree will allow us to take the measurements of an uninterpreted region and calculate its probable interpretation from a finite list of interpretations on the basis of the learnt knowledge. Exercise 5.5 concerns the derivation of a classification tree.

More specifically, we shall have a *region classification tree*. In the following, call the possible interpretations (plate, fork, etc.) $I_1, I_2, \dots I_p \dots I_m$ and the regions $R_1, R_2 \dots R_i \dots R_r$. The classification tree will allow explicit values to be assigned to the expressions

$$Pr(R_i \text{ has interpretation } I_p)$$

It is important to note that these probabilities are calculated *conditional* on the associated feature measurements; in probability theory terms, we are determining

$$Pr(R_i \text{ is } I_p \mid measurements \text{ of } R_i) \qquad 5.9$$

A crude idea would be to assign meanings to regions on the basis of which interpretation had the highest probability 5.9. If we had chosen "good" features with which to describe the regions, this might yield an accurate interpretation of the scene - we can even derive an expression that yields a "probability" of our interpretation being correct; suppose that interpretation I_{p_i} has been assigned to region R_i - then

$$Pr(interpretation) = \qquad 5.10$$

$$\prod_i Pr(R_i \text{ is } I_{p_i} \mid measurements \text{ of } R_i)$$

Our crude algorithm aims to maximise 5.10 by maximising the individual terms of the product.

A rather more intelligent idea is to recognise that the regions will not be independent of each other. In particular, *neighbouring* regions will exhibit features of interaction that we may be able to observe easily, and their common boundaries will have features that we can measure. For example, in our dinner table picture, plate regions will normally be adjacent to table regions; table/floor boundaries may be expected to be longer than fork/table boundaries. Many other domain specific features will suggest themselves, allowing a *boundary classification tree* to be built from the known segmentations much as the region classification tree was. Now, writing B_{ij} for the common boundary between neighbouring regions R_i and R_j, an improvement on 5.10 is

$$Pr(interpretation) = \qquad\qquad\qquad 5.11$$

$$\prod_i Pr(R_i \text{ is } I_{p_i} \mid measurements \, of \, R_i) \times$$

$$\prod_{ij} Pr(B_{ij} \text{ is between } I_{p_i} \text{ and } I_{p_j} \mid measurements \, of \, B_{ij})$$

The probabilities of the second part of the product will be calculated from the boundary classification tree. Unfortunately this improved model will not maximise $Pr(interpretation)$ simply by taking the best region estimates since this will not necessarily maximise the boundary probabilities; the interaction of neighbouring regions means that we have to assign meanings with more thought and a new algorithm is required.

In fact, given boundary probabilities, we are in a position to combine the merging and interpretation processes thereby deriving a segmentation based not only on pure "image" properties, but incorporating domain based knowledge which, we hope, will have a better idea of what "regions" actually are in the context of the image. The idea will be to take a crude segmentation as a starting point - perhaps by applying the region grower described earlier with thresholds chosen to leave the job incomplete; further region merging will be on the basis of semantic knowledge, and this first phase only serves to cut down the amount of necessary work. Now if two regions R_i and R_j are separated by a boundary B_{ij} we can calculate a probability of B_{ij} being "real" by noting that boundaries in the image must separate two regions of *different* interpretation. We have

$$Pr(B_{ij} \text{ separates different interpretations}) = \qquad 5.12$$

$$\sum_{p,q,p<>q} Pr(B_{ij} \text{ is between } I_p, I_q \mid measurements \, of \, B_{ij}) \times$$

$$Pr(R_i \text{ is } I_p \mid measurements \, of \, R_i) \times$$

$$Pr(R_j \text{ is } I_q \mid measurements \, of \, R_j)$$

(This formula is not claimed to be the best possible; see Exercise 5.6 for the derivation of an alternative). These probabilities may then be used to guide the merging. The common boundary with lowest probability would be deleted first as we hope that the low probability gives a better judge of "weakness" than the intensity level measurements used before.

There remains the problem of assigning interpretations to regions in such a way as to maximise 5.11. Ideally, of course, an exhaustive search of *all* possible assignments of interpretations is made, but the computational load of such a scheme will probably be prohibitive. An alternative is to consider each region in isolation as before. We have a value for $Pr(R_i$ is $I_p \mid$ *measurements on* $R_i)$ for all p, $1 \leq p \leq m$, so assume $p = i_1$ gives the largest such probability, $p = i_2$ the next largest, and so on. Then

$$Pr(R_i \text{ is } I_{i_1} \mid measurements \text{ on } R_i) \geq$$

$$Pr(R_i \text{ is } I_{i_2} \mid measurements \text{ on } R_i) \geq$$

$$Pr(R_i \text{ is } I_{i_3} \mid measurements \text{ on } R_i) \geq$$

$$\cdots$$

Now set

$$Conf(R_i \text{ is } I_{i_1}) = \frac{Pr(R_i \text{ is } I_{i_1} \mid measurements \text{ on } R_i)}{Pr(R_i \text{ is } I_{i_2} \mid measurements \text{ on } R_i)}$$

Proceed by finding the region with the largest value of the confidence ratio $Conf(i)$, and taking its implied best interpretation as correct. Having done this, we can amend the probabilities of all regions *neighbouring* R_i by observing that the boundaries they have with the now *interpreted* region will influence their own interpretation probabilities. Suppose that region R_j has a common boundary B_{ij} with region R_i; we will update the probabilities associated with region R_j as follows

$$Pr_{new}(R_j \text{ is } I_p) = Pr_{old}(R_j \text{ is } I_p) \times$$

$$Pr(B_{ij} \text{ separates regions } I_p, I_{i_1} \mid measurements \text{ of } B_{ij})$$

after which the confidence ratios $Conf(j)$ can be recalculated for each affected region R_j. The new confidence ratios will have incorporated the decision to allocate an interpretation to R_i, and we can now assign an interpretation to the region with the next highest value of $Conf$.

Iterating this scheme will assign interpretations to all regions and provide at least a local maximum for the overall interpretation probability 5.11. One use of this approximation to 5.11 may be to guide the halting of the region merging procedure; it is fair to expect that the value of 5.11 derived from a segmentation with too many boundaries will be smaller than one derived from the correct segmentation, while (likewise) if there are too *few* boundaries (so the merging has gone too far), 5.11 will yield a probability less than that given by the best segmentation. One application of the algorithm may then be to derive a value for 5.11 for every putative segmentation in the merging process until the value passes a (local) maximum.

It should be observed that the interpretation itself may imply a region merging; if two neighbouring regions are given the same interpretation as a result of the confidence ratio assignments, we may reasonably remove the boundary between them. Such a process (Feldman & Yakimovsky, 1974) has successfully recognised areas of "grass" in an image, even though the shade of the grass varied through brown, green and yellow, and any unintelligent region merger would have left false boundaries intact. It should also be observed that we have no guarantee of the best interpretation; we cannot be sure that the segmentation is the correct one, or that for a given segmentation 5.11 has been maximised.

It is not suggested that the use of the probabilities described here is the best possible - one possible different strategy would be to measure boundary strength by evaluating our estimate of 5.11 before and after a boundary removal, aiming to remove boundaries that maximised the probability; this would be a very time consuming alternative to using 5.11, but there is nothing to say that this idea would be any better or worse. Our underlying assumption throughout has been that region interpretations depend only on the region and its immediate neighbours - relaxing this assumption to allow an interpreted region to influence the probabilities of *all* other regions is of course a possibility, but implies prohibitive computational cost.

The Intelligence of Segmentation Techniques

Various ways of segmenting an image have been presented in this chapter; some are unsophisticated and could equally well be applied to all classes of image, others make some assumptions about the scene represented or go looking for specific features. We should stress that the ideas we have looked at are merely a selection from a wide range of segmentation techniques, a selection designed to give a flavour of the task.

The algorithms have developed from the simplest pixel-based ideas, through the interaction of regions to the incorporation of semantics; especially for the last algorithm presented, it should be clear that we have moved well away from Image Processing and into Artificial Intelligence. The semantic region grower and interpreter, despite its crude model of the world, its inherently unreliable approximations and probable horrendous computational cost and unwieldy learning phase, represents a *knowledge based* approach that does much more than just play with intensity levels. Of course, the quality of the results achieved will depend on the quality of the semantic model; we have to be sure that the features we measure and use to guide the segmentation do indeed differentiate between regions of different interpretation. Other workers (Tenenbaum & Barrow, 1977) have used similar ideas elaborated with region constraints (such as "a plate will be connected to a table" or "a bottle will not be connected to a chair"). They then use the idea of *constraint propagation* further to restrict region interpretations. More recently (Tailor et al., 1987) successful segmentation programs have been written that identify regions in satellite images, guided by a knowledge base that is a computerised map of the area of the image. If prior information of this sort of quality about the image is already known then we can apply "intelligence" to the segmentation that is an order of magnitude greater than anything described hitherto.

This sort of approach represents the future for Vision systems - we shall expect to see segmentation algorithms that pass their first approximations to some knowledgeable part of the system that will in turn provide feedback based on domain dependent knowledge, and permit intelligent updates to the segmentation (Ohta 1985) (these ideas will be explored further in Chapter 10). Notice in particular that nothing has been said hitherto about three dimensional information being incorporated; when we realise that the two dimensional scene has to be interpreted in terms of three dimensional objects, it should be clear that some "knowledgeable" feedback is going to be essential to any reliable interpretation.

Exercises

(1) How might a histogram approach be used to segment an image representing *two* objects, of different intensity on a non-uniform background?

(2) Suggest how Prager's relaxation algorithm, described in the text, may be improved by considering edges further from a particular edge than its immediate (adjacent) neighbours.
     Do you think such a scheme would be useful in practice?

(3) Implement the hierarchical edge detector listed in Appendix I. Amend it to count the calls it makes to the primitive edge operator, and use this to gauge its efficiency for various heights of pyramid and edge magnitude thresholds.

(4) Suggest how the Hough transform technique for circle hunting outlined in the text could be amended to introduce *weighted* incrementing of the

accumulator array when refining the algorithm with edge direction information.

(5)   List the features you might use, and how you might quantify them, to classify the regions in a scene of cars on a road in countryside for use by a semantic region grower.

(6)   Equation 5.12 is not the best estimate of this probability; better might be

$$Pr(false) = \frac{P_f}{P_t + P_f} \qquad\qquad 5.13$$

where P_t is the probability deduced in 5.12 and P_f is the probability that B_{ij} is between two subregions of the same interpretation. $P(false)$ then gives the probability of the boundary being *false*.

Deduce a formula for P_f and justify the formula for $P(false)$.

[Formulae of the shape of 5.13 are common in conditional probability analysis, and often appear in Artificial Intelligence applications, for example (Atwell & Elliot, 1987) .]

CHAPTER 6

A PCB example

Printed Circuit Boards

A printed circuit board (PCB) can be found almost anywhere electronic components are used. They enable components to be mounted on a flat board with connections between them etched, or printed, on the surface. Sizes vary from a centimetre square to a few tens of centimetres on the longest side. Automatic inspection of boards has been achieved (Hara et al, 1983).

Once an electronic circuit has been designed, it needs to be converted into a layout on a PCB. It is common to use a CAD system for this, but sometimes a layout is constructed manually. The end result is the PCB *artwork* plus associated documentation; an example of artwork is shown on the left of Figure 6.1 - the actual size of this would be about 1.5 centimetres square. The straight black lines are called *tracks* and serve as (electrical) connections between components which usually sit on the *pads* depicted as circles. Pads commonly have drills holed in them; there could be other holes required for the physical securing of components. There may be hundreds or even thousands of holes, each drilled to an accuracy of typically 0.025mm relative to some datum; there may be about half a dozen different drill sizes on a single PCB.

Manufacture of a PCB takes several stages. For our purposes, the important one is the programming of a machine tool to drill holes to fit the artwork which is etched onto the board, usually at a later stage. There may be other cutting operations such as routing a smooth edge around the board. The obvious source of data to program the machine is the CAD system database, however, for reasons we do not need to explore, the actual artwork is often the source. The artwork is read by a camera mounted near the machine drilling spindle: normally this takes place under the direct control of a fairly skilled operator but this chapter examines some of the scope for Computer Vision to assist this laborious task.

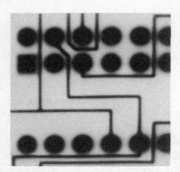 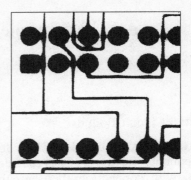

Figure 6.1 PCB artwork, and a segmentation

Gross System Constraints

Consider briefly what the accuracy constraint implies; if we are fortunate and can digitise a frame to a 1024 pixel square image, it should not need much justification to say that the frame cannot be much more than 1cm square. If the pixels at which we look represent significantly more than 0.001cm (or 0.01mm) then by the time quantisation effects and any errors inherent in the algorithms to be used have done their work, there will be no guarantee of 0.025mm accuracy. Now if the board at hand is, say, 10cm square, we need to study 100 frames, each of which will involve substantial processing.

We are also going to face a number of problems in the image acquisition. Before even approaching the artwork, it should be noted that standards vary, so sometimes pads are depicted as circles, at other times as diamonds etc. CAD generated artwork may not show the actual holes in the pads, while hand generated artwork may be inconsistent over the whole area. There may also be errors in the design. The artwork is photographed onto a glossy transparent film which is mounted on the drilling surface so the lighting conditions and the state of the surface may cause reflections, uneveness in the contrast of the image and odd blobs and other blemishes in the background. Together these observations say that while artwork is essentially simple - a collection of circles and straight lines - in practice the circles may be imperfect, circles that represent identical features may vary in diameter, differently generated pictures of the same product may appear very different, and the image that we acquire may have much more spurious information present than may be expected from looking at the original.

Some Simple Algorithms

The simplicity of the images that this application creates make it a good example for illustrating the elementary algorithms we have seen to date.

Thresholding

A PCB represents an object-background scene; a particular pixel may be expected to be ''within'' a track or pad, or to be part of the board background. It should therefore be possible unambiguously to threshold a PCB image and isolate the features of interest as black, leaving the background as white. Figure 6.1 shows an example image, whose intensity histogram is given in Figure 6.2. The histogram is clearly bimodal, although this shows well how choosing precisely the best threshold can be a challenge; an adequate segmentation of the PCB features is achieved by thresholding at the indicated position, although since the orignal image did not provide crisp delineation of the PCB features, we will suffer blurring. The right of Figure 6.1 shows the result of this.

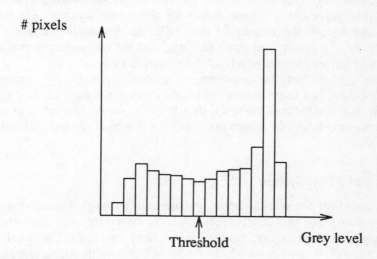

Figure 6.2 PCB image histogram

Segmentation

If the image acquisition is "clean", with even contrast and little or no noise, then quite probably the simple thresholding will be enough to segment the features. We should admit the possibility, though, that the lighting will be unfavourable or that some other kind of corruption may occur, in which case we may choose another low level techniques at this stage.

Circle Detection

The example to hand is a very good one in the sense that what is produced by the low level noise filters and edge detectors is not at all what we want; the information we need is circle centres and radii, and straight line directions and lengths. However perfect the edge detection, the boundaries will still be "stepwise". This information is, though, ideal input for a Hough transform. To illustrate this, consider searching Figure 6.1, which is 512 pixels square, for circles of radius 30 pixels, using as input the edges determined by the simple thresholding. The algorithm applied is exactly as described in the preceding chapter - Figure 6.3 is a "plot" of the contents of the accumulator array in which bright spots represent strong evidence and dark areas represent weak evidence for the circle centres. The brightest points are indeed the centres of the circles in the original image. Notice, though, the "ghosting" of other features, and the rings of evidence near the centres of circles that are nearly of the specified radius.

Notice also that the algorithm does not give totally unambiguous answers; there is a large number of bright spots in the accumulator array that provide marginally less evidence than the true circle centres, and we shall not know automatically which are correct and which are not without further processing.

Outline of a Full System

The location of the tracks can be pursued with Hough Transforms also; in fact we can make this search very swift by observing that the "lines" for which we are looking are horizontal, vertical or inclined at $\pm\pi/4$ radians (other artwork may of course have tracks at other inclinations, but it is common for these to be taken from a small, and certainly finite, set). This significantly reduces the size of the parameter space in which the accumulator array resides. Further, the location of the straight line endpoints is simplified considerably if we already know the position of the pads - most of the tracks join pads together, possibly including some turns through angles chosen from a small set (probably right angles or half right angles).

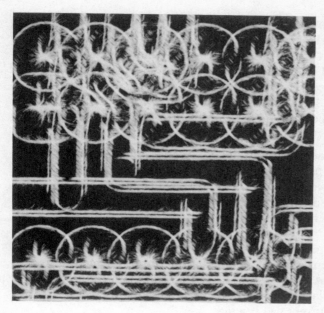

Figure 6.3 A Hough accumulator array

The application also has special features in that, with most artwork, the pads are represented by two *concentric* circles. An intelligent system would certainly make use of this foreknowledge, in particular to rake out spurious evidence where putative pads were not represented by concentric circles, but also to guide and accelerate the algorithms.

It is worth asking what performance we would want from such system. Processing the artwork by manual means can take of the order of an hour on the machine. With a Vision system, we would find a processing elapsed time of several hours acceptable, especially if all the data could be captured in one operation using only a few minutes of drilling machine time. This would involve the storage of the order of 100Mbytes of data for off-line analysis. This requirement is not beyond the bounds of practicality.

Further Ideas

A requirement during the PCB production phase is to test the electrical continuity along tracks between different pads. It is possible to perform an analysis of the tracks to determine which pads are topologically connected (Taylor 1985). The output from the analysis could drive suitable testing procedures. Naturally, CAD generated testing data is preferable when available.

It was mentioned above that there may be various drill sizes. Sometimes, but not always, it is possible to determine the drill size from the context. For example, if the PCB has tracks on both sides, they may be electrically connected *via* a hole plated with a conductor. The size of the hole is different from normal pads. These vias are often placed near integrated circuit packages, or DILs, whose pad pattern consists of two rows of pads at a fixed inter pad distance. It would be possible to deduce the drill size for vias and DILs with rules such as:

IF   the pad is in a pair of straight lines of pads **AND**
     each pad along a line is x mm from it neighbour **AND**
     the two lines are y mm apart and parallel **AND**
     there are the same number of pads in each line
THEN the set of pads is a DIL

IF   the current pad is within the boundary of a DIL **AND**
     the current pad is equidistant from two pads in the
     DIL **AND**
     the distance from these pads is less than z mm
THEN the current pad is a via

IF   the current pad is a DIL pad
THEN drill type is n

IF   the current pad is a via
THEN drill type is m

This sort of construct and its associated control structure is studied in depth in Chapter 10. We could, of course, also consider evidence from the tracks on the reverse side of the PCB were this to be available.

It can be seen that we are starting to allow low level Computer Vision algorithms and much higher level, domain dependent, processing to interact. By domain dependent we mean that we have to find abstract models of the problem we are trying to solve: we need to know roughly what we are looking at. We could take this a step further in order to speed up the scanning process. Some PCBs, such as those for computer memory, employ very regular layouts such as row after row of DILs all of the same size. If we could gather some notion of this high level plan of the layout, the search could be directed more effectively. We would make hypotheses about where to expect DILs and then look for them. Around them we would look to tracks, vias and space.

It is an important point to note that exploiting the model is the best way to design the solution - without knowledge of the features of the object, that the lines are at known orientations and the circles regularly spaced and in concentric pairs, we are left to perform an exhaustive search for interesting features. Using the model we can cut the search space, verify features hitherto isolated and generate information about the nature of the board.

The Need for more Intelligence

While some of the ideas we have express can be implemented using lower level algorithms, more inferencing capabilities are required. It is still too early in the life of Computer Vision to predict with certainty just what the general form of this capability will be, but it is already clear that it will draw on the ideas of Artificial Intelligence.

It can be seen that even in the relatively simple application of PCB artwork, high level processing is needed. However, we should not forget that most problems are far less tractable. The PCB "alphabet" is circles and lines - most problems will have much larger alphabets of objects or subobjects. Much more important, a PCB can be quite adequately examined as a two dimensional image and most serious applications are firmly lodged in the 3D world. Accordingly, we now turn our attention towards 3D model based Vision. As one would expect with the increased complexity, so the intrinsic difficulty of the work increases.

Exercises

(1) What would be the effect of searching a PCB image for circles of radius one or two pixels less than (or more than) the true circle radius?
(2) What would be the effect of choosing the resolution of the PCB image so low as to make the circles of radius three or four pixels?

CHAPTER 7

Line labelling

学美

Introduction

We have seen a variety of ways of dealing with intensity images. These techniques, and others, we hope will lead us to a clean, complete and accurate segmentation - ideally this will be represented by a list of pertinent features (e.g. "square", "ellipse", "line") together with dimensions and position in the image. Provided this information is available, there is already a lot that Computer Vision can do for us - for example the case study of PCB artwork analysis given in the preceding chapter. A limited "alphabet" of features can be reliably detected, allowing various levels of analysis to be performed in looking for defects, connectivity etc. Much the same may be said about a very old application of image analysis and feature recognition - character recognition. If we are provided with typewriter (or other mechanically produced) text then once again it is from a finite, known alphabet and algorithms just such as those presented in the preceding chapters will be adequate for identifying letters from an intensity image. Character recognition is an application with interesting problems - suppose for example that the image is very noisy or, equivalently, the type quality poor. There then may be uncertainties in the character stream we generate from the recognition process. Foreknowledge of the nature of the text (which in our context we may regard as *semantic* information, although this does not imply linguistic semantics) may well then allow us to "fill in the gaps" - a good example of this may be a system that reads time stamp cards. In such an application the alphabet is strictly limited, perhaps just to digits; information will appear in rigid format and there is significant foreknowledge about what is "likely" - for example, clock-in times may be known to be around 0800, while clock-off times may be known to be around 1700. A combination of visually detected features and some elementary A.I. techniques, ideally with some feedback from the second to first, would be able to do a very respectable job.

Most applications of course are far from this level of simplicity. The most conspicuous omission from our considerations to date has been the fact that the images are *two dimensional* representations of a *three dimensional* world. How to elicit three dimensional information from two is a very

88

difficult problem in Computer Vision that preoccupies much of current research work. We might observe that an image is a projection of a piece of three dimensional space (or three-space) onto a piece of two-space. What we want to do is to invert the projection, but since we have lost a dimension in the projection, this inversion is going to be non-unique unless we put constraints on the three space features that we will admit, or somehow else acquire more information than one image will provide.

Much of the remainder of this book examines the problem of getting three dimensional information. This is an active area of research and the "right" answers are not known - some of the ideas used are simple, some are complicated indeed. In this chapter we begin with an idea first formulated in 1963 (Roberts 1965) which is limited in many ways, and regarded as somewhat old fashioned. It does however provide a flavour for what can be done under some assumptions, and for how difficult three dimensional Vision is.

Block Worlds

Roberts postulates a world of *blocks* - specifically he requires that all objects be composed of combinations of three "primitives", shown in Figure 7.1. By scaling and rotating selections of these, we can create a range of three dimensional objects. Arguably we can approximate *any* object to any desired precision by taking enough of these primitives (and making then. small enough) but it is worth observing that in industrial applications, a large number of components could be described in this sort of manner quite simply.

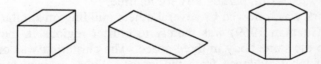

Figure 7.1 The primitives of Roberts´ world

There is a large leap of faith implied here; we are going to assume that the two dimensional images which we are going to explore for information have been segmented accurately *and* completely. This is far from easy - consider for example the simple image shown in Figure 5.15, and its associated edge detections shown in Figure 7.2. The first of these is a Sobel edge detection and the second has used a hierarchical technique. In order to pull out evidence of all the edges it is necessary to reduce thresholds so far as to incur a lot of noise. While it would be possible to rake this out (since it does not represent a "feature" satisfying our constraint) it is still unclear that the cube edges that are not part of its silhouette are indeed straight lines. *Human* perception has no difficulty in filling in these gaps; no more will be said about this point here beyond remarking that it is a very real problem.

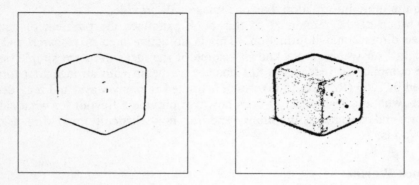

Figure 7.2 Two edge detections of Figure 5.15

Roberts' program proceeded by identifying image features (bounded regions, or vertices at which several boundaries meet) that probably represented a part of one of the primitives. This identification would then be reinforced or abandoned by locating (or not) the other relevant features of the primitive. Upon complete identification, a primitive is "removed" from the image and another one searched for in what remains. The program was remarkably successful, particularly for its time.

This work was followed by several others building on similar ideas. One approach (Guzman 1969) was merely to cluster regions in the image that belonged to the same body in three-space. The clustering was performed on the basis of local evidence from the image - links are introduced between regions to reinforce the chance that they belong to the same body; also some inhibitory links could be introduced to indicate that two regions probably did not belong to the same body. Guzman discovered that this approach results in a mass of special cases, and the resulting program is not very elegant. It is not clear that this idea helps us (or machines) to "understand" three-space, or how it should be analysed.

Line Labelling

An elaboration of Guzman's ideas was developed independently by two different researchers (Clowes 1971, Huffman 1971). Rather than merely identify which regions were connected in three-space, they attempted to assign "meaning" (convex, concave, occluding) to all the edges. Clowes and Huffman's ideas are similar - we shall examine Clowes' approach in more detail.

Clowes supposes that the world is occupied only by objects whose faces are *planar* and *polygonal*, and that no more than three such faces meet at any one vertex. A projection of such a body into two dimensions will provide an image which may be segmented into polygonal regions, and whose vertices are the meeting of either two or three edges.

We distinguish now between the *scene domain* (the "real world", in three dimensions) and the *picture domain* (the image, in two dimensions). In the picture domain, we can see that vertices appear as one of four *Types* (*I*,...,*IV*), illustrated in Figure 7.3. It is convenient to label these regions and edges (the Clowes technique is often referred to as *Line Labelling*) - we adopt the convention of labelling the "biggest" region *A*, and then the other(s) *B* (and *C*) in a clockwise fashion. The edges are labelled *a*, *b* (and *c*) clockwise at the same time. The "biggest" region is unambiguous for ELL, ARROW and TEE junctions, but for FORK is chosen arbitrarily.

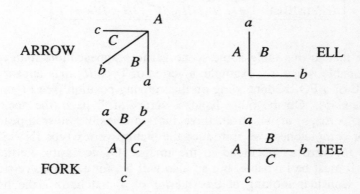

Figure 7.3 The four vertex types

In the scene domain, an edge of a solid body (that satisfies our constraints) must be convex or concave, but never, of course, both. Since each scene vertex is a meeting of three faces, it must also be a meeting point of three edges, so we may classify them as in Table 7.1. Of the three faces that meet at a vertex, 0, 1, 2 or 3 may actually be visible - we subcategorise scene domain vertices according to this number, thereby getting sixteen scene domain vertex Types in all, I_0, I_1, I_2, ..., IV_2, IV_3.

Table 7.1

Type I	3 convex edges
Type II	2 convex edges, 1 concave edge
Type III	1 convex edge, 2 concave edges
Type IV	3 concave edges

When we ask how a *scene* vertex may appear as a *picture* vertex, we see that the possibilities listed in Table 7.2 occur.

Table 7.2

Picture	Scene
ELL	I_1, II_1, II_2, III_3
ARROW	I_2, II_3, III_4
FORK	I_3, II_2, IV_3
TEE	I_2, II_2
INVISIBLE	I_0, II_0, III_0, IV_0, III_1, IV_2, IV_1

Observe that in this table some scene vertices appear more than once - this is reasonable, since, for example, a vertex of Type II_2 may appear as an ELL, a TEE or a FORK depending on the viewing position (see Figure 7.4, vertices 4 and 5). On the other hand, a vertex of Type I (the apex of a tetrahedron, perhaps) at which all three faces are visible *must* appear as a FORK. For completeness we introduce the picture vertex type INVISIBLE to account for vertices occluded in the image. Of necessity, vertices of "subtype" 0 must be invisible, but so also will be, for example, vertices of Type IV_1. Consider looking at the interior of a matchbox - the bottom corners are of Type IV. If only one of the faces that meet at a given corner is visible, the corner itself must be hidden too. Figure 7.4 and Table 7.3 illustrate some of these categorisations.

We now have a correspondence between real vertices and observed vertices - for a given picture each vertex will have a number of possible interpretations. What we are looking for are interpretations that are mutually compatible; this is achieved by inspecting the nature of the edges that link pairs of vertices. We know that in the scene domain a particular edge

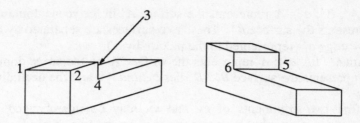

Figure 7.4 Two views of a solid

separates two regions and is either convex or concave. In the picture domain an edge still separates two regions, but in the scene domain the surfaces that these regions represent may be connected by the edge, *or* the edge may be a silhouetting edge and one of the regions will be "behind" the other. Notice at this point that some picture vertices will not correspond to real scene vertices, but are the result of occlusions; characteristically these will cause TEE junctions. Vertex 3 in Figure 7.4 is such a junction.

Table 7.3

Number	2-D	3-D
1	ARROW	I_2
2	FORK	I_3
3	TEE	non-junction
4	ELL	II_2
5	FORK	II_2
6	ARROW	II_3

Adopt notation as follows; A, B, C, ... will be regions in the picture domain, and a,b,c, ... will be edges joining two such regions. A', B', C', ... will be surfaces in the scene domain, and likewise a', b', c', ... will be lines joining two such surfaces. For a given scene vertex, it is possible that some of its associated surfaces and lines will not be visible - adopt the convention of labelling these X', Y', Z' and x', y', z'. Given a picture domain vertex at which edges a, b, c separate regions A, B, C we now introduce three predicates to describe the lines meeting at that vertex as an interpretation of a scene domain junction.

(1) $vx(A', B', a')$: A represents the surface A' in the scene domain and B represents the surface B'. These two surfaces are separated by the *convex* edge a' (represented in the picture by a).

(2)   **cv**(A', B', a'): A represents the surface A' in the scene domain and B
represents the surface B'. These two surfaces are separated by the *concave* edge a' (represented in the picture by a).

(3)   **hind**(A', B', a'): A represents the surface A' in the scene domain and
B represents the surface B'. B' lies *behind* A', and the occluding edge
is a'.

The first two arguments of **cv** and **vx** may be interchanged without
affecting their meaning, but the same is not of course true of **hind**.

An example of these predicates in action may make them clearer. Consider the ARROW vertex v that is the peak of the tetrahedron shown in Figure 7.5 - interpreting it as it is (of scene Type I_2) then the largest region (A)
forms the background in the three dimensional interpretation. We would
describe it as

    vx(B', X', a')
    vx(B', C', b')
    vx(C', X', c')
    hind(B', A', a')
    hind(C', A', c')

Notice it has been necessary to introduce a hidden surface X' to complete the
description of the vertex. Alternatively an ARROW may represent a junction of scene Type II_3 - for instance the junction labelled 6 in Figure 7.4. In
this case the description would be

    vx(A', B', a')
    vx(A', C', c')
    cv(B', C', b')

We may now list exhaustively the possible interpretations of any picture
vertex - this list is given in Appendix III. It defines twenty three different
types of vertex, of which three are ARROW, six are ELL, five are FORK,
five are TEE and four are INVISIBLE. One of the TEE junctions actually
has the same three dimensional interpretation as one of the ARROWS, so
there are twenty two distinct junctions here. For convenience they are allo-
cated canonical type numbers, 1 ... 22.

Now when confronted with an uninterpreted image, we can exploit this
list to derive a "coherent" description of the scene. What follows is a sim-
plification of the full process, for which the interested reader is referred to
the original reference (Clowes 1971), but the principle should be clear.
Essentially the algorithm goes through two stages.

During stage 1, for an arbitrary vertex, choose a valid interpretation from
the table given in Appendix III. This interpretation forces the edges at that
vertex to be one of **cv**, **vx** or **hind**; the key to the scheme is to observe that
this edge must be of the the same type *at its other end*. This is intuitively

clear - it is hard to imagine a polyhedral solid whose edges begin convex and end up concave, or which are occluding (silhouette) edges at one end and not at the other. This most important point allows us to inspect the neighbouring vertices and ask which interpretations are valid in the light of our knowledge about the connecting edge. It is possible that there will still be more than one valid interpretation at such neighbouring vertices, but the idea can be used to propagate the interpretation through the image. Either we will confront a contradiction (a vertex has no valid interpretation from the table in Appendix III in the light of what we have assumed about some of its incident edges) or an (edgewise) coherent interpretation will emerge for all vertices.

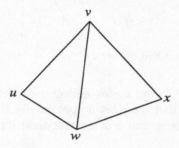

Figure 7.5 A tetrahedron

Stage two of the algorithm takes adjacent vertex pairs and determines the boundaries of faces. It is important to note that any "interpretations" generated by stage one are not necessarily going to provide a coherent three dimensional interpretation. We have only obliged neighbouring vertices to have the same ideas about the intervening edge. The second stage of the algorithm ensures that all around the boundary of all regions there is continuous consistency. Specifically, Clowes allows a set of vertices to define a surface boundary if:

1. any picture vertex appears at most once in the set;
2. any node that does so appear has precisely one interpretation in the table in Appendix III;
3. the nodes (and their joining arcs) are cyclically ordered.

The first condition here ensures "figure of eight" paths do not appear as face boundaries, while the second ensures that on returning to the starting point of an edge loop, the first vertex does not change interpretation.

Example

By way of example we shall derive an interpretation of the picture in Figure
7.5. This image has four vertices, two of which are ARROW and two of
which are ELL.

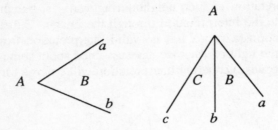

Figure 7.6 An ELL and an ARROW vertex

Referring to Figure 7.6, and remembering the labelling *local* to each vertex, consider one of the ELL vertices u; potentially this is of canonical type
4, 5, 6, 7, 8, or 9. Suppose that it is of canonical type 7; then we have the
interpretation

> vx(A', X', a')
> vx(A', B', b')
> cv(B', X', x')
> hind(A', B', a')

Remembering this, consider vertex v (Figures 7.5, 7.6). We are required to
find an interpretation that puts region C *behind* region A (with respect to
line c) since B is behind A with respect to line a at the ELL vertex; no possible ARROW interpretation permits this and we have a contradiction. Vertex u therefore cannot be of canonical type 7.

Alternatively, if we suppose that u is of canonical type 4 we have the
interpretation

> vx(B', X', a')
> vx(B', Y', b')
> vx(X', Y', x')
> hind(B', A', a')
> hind(B', A', b')

Constraining A to be behind B with respect to a at the ELL vertex con-
strains A to be behind C with respect to c at the ARROW vertex - the only
possible such interpretation is for the ARROW (vertex v) to be of canonical
type 1.

Propagating this reasoning tells us that if vertex v is of canonical type 1, vertex x must be of canonical type 4 or 8, while if vertex w is of canonical type 1, vertex x must be of canonical type 4 or 9. The only conclusion, given the original assumption, is that vertex x is of canonical type 4, and we have the interpretation of a "floating tetrahedron" - that is, it is not resting on the surface A.

It should be stressed that a different original assumption about vertex u may have led to a different interpretation - in particular the picture may represent a tetrahedron resting on the base A (and so the edges joining u to w and w to x would be *concave*). There is no way without more information that we could distinguish between these cases. The challenge of making the interpretation search "efficient" is a general consistent labelling problem (Haralick & Shapiro, 1979, Mackworth 1977) which can be abstracted and applied to many domains. We desire, of course, to minimise the number of blind alleys (contradictions) we encounter, and thus reduce the backtracking work in finding a consistent interpretation.

Observations

A number of conclusions can be drawn about the scheme we have described - most obvious perhaps are its serious limitations. There are not many applications one can think of that are truly limited to objects satisfying Clowes' criteria of planar, polygonal surfaces, with three meeting at each vertex. As has been remarked, we might approximate any object with solids satisfying these criteria but this hardly seems a satisfactory long term strategy for solving Vision problems. In point of fact, Clowes' algorithm has serious problems even when it is only dealing with the simplest objects if they happen to be in unfortunate positions. There are some instances of this in Figure 7.7 - vertices appear to have more than three edges leading into them. In fact this sort of thing can be detected as a special case, and the algorithm will survive - the point of restricting vertices to be the junction of three edges is to reduce the search space and number of line and vertex labels.

Much more serious is the constraint that surfaces must be planar and edges straight. It is obvious just by looking around that very few objects actually fall into this category, and a world composed solely of them would be limited indeed. Any relaxation of this constraint would cause considerable extra complication since the relations *convex* or *concave* could apply to surfaces as well as to the edges joining them - there is also the possibility that two surfaces could become coplanar at their shared edge. Most serious, we are no longer guaranteed that a picture edge actually represents a scene edge - consider a sphere whose circular outline does not represent an edge, circular or otherwise.

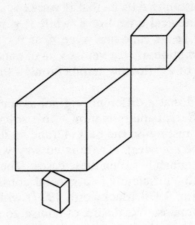

Figure 7.7 Some apparently juxtaposed solids

We might consider exactly with which solids (or "solids") this scheme will succeed. Interestingly, "impossible" objects such as Figure 7.8 will not match any three-space scene; the algorithm will fail because what is wrong with the picture (it is impossible to maintain interpretations of vertices/edges on a circuit of a region) is exactly what the program exploits. Conversely, Figure 7.9 *will* cause a three-space interpretation to be generated; the lines and vertices are quite all right, but it is impossible to build such a figure in three-space within the constraint of *planar* surfaces.

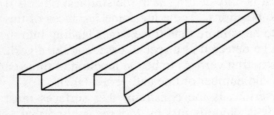

Figure 7.8 An "impossible object" that will not be accepted

The ideas described in this chapter are just the beginning of a whole area of effort to understand "line drawings". Extensions to the ideas described have attempted, for example, to incorporate illumination information by trying to identify shadows (Waltz 1975). Waltz also permitted vertices to be the junction of up to four lines. The resulting program can label lines in nearly 100 ways, and the number of possible vertex labels multiplies enormously. Interestingly, the result of this is that, as more information is coded into the labels, the number of possible meaningful interpretations at any particular vertex goes down. Further, the constraints imposed on neighbouring vertices are also considerably stronger, and the expected "combinatorial explosion" does not occur.

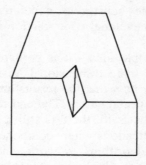

Figure 7.9 An "impossible object" that will be accepted

In an attempt to cater for pictures such as Figure 7.9 another approach (Mackworth 1973) attempted to derive information about the planar faces rather than the edges of the bodies we admit. Each face is a subplane of a well defined plane in 3-space, given by an equation such as

$$a_x x + a_y y + a_z z + 1 = 0$$

We are already familiar with the idea of *parameter spaces* and it should be clear that such a plane can be represented as the point (a_x, a_y, a_z) in a dual space. Two planes in "real" space are represented by two points in dual space, and the line that is their intersection in real space is represented by the line joining the two points in dual space. Mackworth supposed that the image plane was $z=0$ (the xy plane), and exploited a particular subspace of this dual called *gradient space*, which may be thought of as the plane G given by $a_z=1$ in the dual space. A point in dual space is mapped onto the gradient space plane by determining the intersection of the line joining it to the origin with G - it is not hard to see that the co-ordinates of this intersection point are $(\dfrac{a_x}{a_z}, \dfrac{a_y}{a_z}, 1)$, giving gradient space co-ordinates

$$(G_x, G_y) = (\frac{a_x}{a_z}, \frac{a_y}{a_z})$$

Gradient space has several interesting and useful properties - see Exercise 7.4 and its solution for more details. The general thrust of Mackworth's approach is now that the constraints are geometric coherence rather than junction labels.

We have made many mentions of *constraints* in explaining these ideas; it is worth observing at this point that what we have here is a simple application of the Artificial Intelligence technique known as *constraint propagation*. A hypothesis generates constraints, which reduce the search space over the rest of the data. If no eventual contradiction is derived, then we have a "match".

Line labelling is a simple idea - it is perhaps the way that one might approach the problem of three dimensional Vision as a first attempt. It should be clear though by now that the results are limited and fraught with problems in overcoming special cases. The end result too is likely to admit "impossible objects". That said, there is still a use for these ideas in, for example, engineering applications where components may indeed be as simple as required for the algorithms to work, and furthermore an explicit description of them may be available from machine readable technical drawings. More general results in three dimensions, however, will demand a different approach entirely.

Exercises

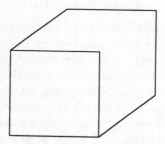

Figure 7.10 An imperfect line image

(1)   Using the technique in the text, exhaust all possible interpretations of Figure 7.5.

(2)   Suppose we restrict Clowes' block world even further to admit objects only with *convex* edges. Generate versions of Tables 7.2 and III.1 (in

Appendix III) for this restricted world.

(3)   A picture of a cube is taken and an edge detector and boundary finder generate the image shown in Figure 7.10; one edge is missing as a result of unfavourable lighting. Demonstrate that Clowes' algorithm does not recognise a "solid" in this image.

What refinements may be put into the algorithm to help?

(4)   Give a geometrical description of gradient space (defined in the text); that is, what is the interpretation of a point particularly near to or remote from the origin of G?

Consider superimposing G on the picture plane. What can you say about the lines in G that correspond to particular line segments in the picture?

CHAPTER 8

Towards Three Dimensions

Introduction

It should be clear after reading Chapter 7 that making three dimensional observations from a single two dimensional image is, in anything except the most specific cases, going to be very hard without some further information about the scene or its contents. This was recognised very early in the development of Vision systems, and consequently several techniques have been developed to help. Some of these use a 2D image (or images) as a starting point and exploit knowledge of the surrounding world; others use different technologies to generate three dimensional information directly.

Once 3D co-ordinates are available the Vision problem is still far from solved. Accordingly this chapter concludes with some remarks about how, given thorough knowledge of the scene, identification of the objects in it may be approached.

Shape from ...

How can the very difficult problem of moving from a 2-space image to 3-space co-ordinates be solved? In Chapter 7 we saw a solution that on balance is very unsuitable that solved the problem by severely limiting the nature of the "real world". An alternative is to make assumptions or know some properties of the scene, or acquire more information by collecting multiple images. There is a variety of properties that may be exploited to derive "shape", or *depth data*, that collectively give rise to a class of algorithms called "*Shape from ...*" - what follows will not be an exhaustive account of such algorithms, but will touch on the major approaches. One of the best known and most successful ideas will be inspected in more detail.

Shape from Shading

It was pointed out at the end of Chapter 7 (Waltz 1975) that knowledge of the lighting model can be a valuable aid in determining shape. Waltz used clues from shadows to augment deductions drawn from assumptions about

102

the structure of the world (that is, polyhedral planar solids). In fact, *shading* can provide a lot of information about more general world scenes (Horn 1975, Ikeuchi & Horn, 1981). Elementary physics (the *reflectance model*), when used in conjunction with some reasonable assumptions about the scene (pixels in the same region, or on the same surface, are usually "smoothly connected") can produce a lot of information about surface orientation in three dimensions.

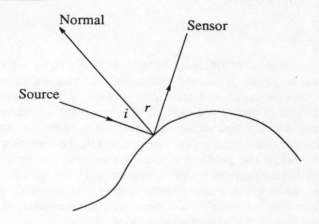

Figure 8.1 Angles of incidence (i) and emittance (r)

What is important in this context is knowledge of the angles of *incidence* (at what angle light from the source(s) strikes the surface, or strictly speaking, at what angle to the surface normal) and *emittance* (at what angle the light leaves the surface for the eye/camera) - there are well known relationships between these determined by properties of the surface (see Figure 8.1, which shows a section through a surface with an incident source and an observer). In particular, the *reflectivity function* is defined for surfaces - for instance if the surface is matte this function varies with the cosine of the incident angle, indicating that the most light is reflected when the source is normal to the surface. On the other hand, mirror like (*specular*) surfaces, such as polished metal, reflect only at an angle of reflection equal to the angle of incidence. The amount of light received by the sensor thus depends on the reflectivity function (the nature of the surface), the angle of incidence and the angle of emittance.

With sufficient knowledge about the surfaces in view and the lighting model, recovery of surface normal directions is now possible. The actual attack may be performed in several ways, but relaxation techniques exploiting probable local "smoothness" (Ikeuchi 1980) and inspection of gradient space (Horn 1975) have both proved successful. (Gradient space is defined and introduced in Chapter 7).

Shading issues would be of considerable value in analysing the dinner table scene discussed in Chapter 1 and shown in Figure 1.1; it should be clear that the reflectance properties of glass, crockery, cutlery and tablecloth are very different from one another and open to exploitation. These issues are also discussed in Chapter 9.

Shape from Texture

"Texture", in the context of intensity images, is likely to be a property of three dimensional surfaces. If correctly identified in an image it can provide strong clues to the orientation and depth of a surface; if a "known" texture is observed in an image then any distortion will be a result of either distance (markings appear smaller and closer together on a receding surface) or curvature/inclination (markings appear compressed in the direction of incli- nation) (Witkin 1981). The problem is to find a suitable description of tex- ture that is sensitive to projection and simultaneously computable from an intensity image. Even given texture identification it is probable that there will be more than one "correct" three dimensional interpretation, and the problem becomes one of choosing the most likely.

Texture may be attacked from various points; we may search the image for texture "primitives" - a picture of a brick wall has obvious rectangular primitives (or rather, quadrilateral primitives if the wall, and hence the rec- tangles, are not normal to the viewer) while a pile of coins will reduce to circular/elliptical primitives. A unit thus of texture has been termed a *texel* (Kender 1978). Alternatively, we may inspect texture from a *syntactic* point of view - grammars can be successfully defined to describe combinations and deformations of textures (Gonzalez & Thomason, 1978). Syntactic approaches are described further in Chapter 9.

From the point of view of shape extraction, the most direct approach is to determine the *texture gradient* - this gradient is the direction of maximum rate of change of size of a projected texture primitive and can provide obvi- ous information about the orientation of observed surfaces. Further if a texel is of known shape (eg, circular), then its perceived shape (elliptical) provides direct clues about the orientation of the surface on which it lies. (Figures 1.1 and 4.13 illustrate how circular primitives (plates) can give rise to a variety of ellipses). If the observed scene contains long parallel lines (regular blocks of buildings for example), their perceived convergence give the per- spective "vanishing points", and hence immediate three dimensional con- text (Kender 1978).

Shape from Motion

The study of motion in images is a large topic about which books have been written, notably Ullman (Ullman 1979), and this book will not endeavour to study it in any detail at all.

In general terms, we remember that a "scene", or image, is a digitised representation of a continuous intensity variation in the world in view; we may observe that this scene is in general changing as the objects in view, or the observer, or both, move with respect to each other, giving rise to *Optical Flow*. Optical flow associates a two dimensional velocity with each point on the 2D image plane; Shape from Motion algorithms attempt to determine the optical flow as a first step, and derive shape from it. Intuitively, it should be clear that, especially if the velocity of the observer is known, the optical flow will reveal surface information in some detail. The mathematics, while not simple, are straightforward but not a part of this book. Exercise 8.1 suggests how optical flow may be deduced.

It is possible that instead of a "large" number of images simulating smooth flow, we have a relatively small number of images displaying moving objects or representing a scene from the point of view of a moving observer - for instance, a camera may be triggered to capture an image every two seconds as a car passes a junction. In these image sequences, continuous optical flow will not be as accessible. Instead we may locate in each image features or points and try to *match* them with particular points in other images of the sequence - this is the *correspondence problem* which we shall see below in studying Shape from Stereo. Algorithms exist (Barnard & Thompson 1979) that solve this problem successfully using relaxation techniques. We remark in passing that the ideas are just as applicable to the stereo correspondence problem as to resolving motion in image sequences.

It is common in analysing motion to assume real world constraints such as rigidity (or at least "piecewise rigidity") - there is some evidence that the human visual system makes this assumption too. Given this assumption, Ullman (Ullman 1979) managed to prove a powerful result which he calls the *Structure from Motion* theorem;

> Given three orthographic projections of four [labelled] non-coplanar points in rigid configuration, the structure and motion compatible with the three views are uniquely determined up to a reflection about the image plane.

or, more colloquially, if we have three images of four rigidly related points, and the correspondences between the points *are known*, then there is essentially only one interpretation we can put on the points and their motion.

We should emphasise here that Ullman's theorem supposes *orthographic* projection (that is, light travelling in parallel rays from objects to image plane), while optical flow will probably exploit the polar projection. There are points of some subtlety here which we shall not explore further (Marr 1982, Ullman 1979).

Shape from Stereo

Human depth perception is an extremely sophisticated business. Our brains will certainly use input based on motion, texture and shading and combine it with contextual information (a "knowledge base") to let us refine comprehensive 3D information about what we see. Surely however the most predominant feature, superficially at any rate, of the human visual system is the fact that we have two eyes and thus perform "stereo vision" (stereopsis). This has been realised for a very long time indeed, and has resulted in the last century in the well known Victorian "stereoscopes" and progressed to the "3D movies", of uncertain success, in the 1950s. The idea has always been that if the two eyes are presented with a slightly different view (a *disparity*), the illusion of three dimensions can be achieved. Conversely, if we view a 3D scene then the eyes are receiving slightly different inputs, so the brain should be able to exploit this to determine depth. It is an obvious experiment to try to mimic this with two cameras.

It is tempting to suppose that binocular vision is essential for our comprehensive visual perception, but it may be worth noting that this may not necessarily be the case. Both Colin Milburn (a wicket keeper) and Gordon Banks (a goal keeper) suffered the loss of one eye and supposed they would have to give up their specialised activities, which demand what the sportsman calls "a good eye", but in point of fact is usually taken to mean two good eyes. That is, they needed very quickly to be able to perceive moving objects and their distance from the viewer accurately and against a variety of backgrounds. That they were able to continue in their respective sports indicates that two eyes are not essential, and that we can train ourselves to cope with just the other clues.

The pioneering work on stereo machine Vision was performed by Marr and Poggio (Marr 1982, Marr & Poggio, 1979) and it is their algorithm which we have chosen to describe in detail. It should be stressed, however, that this is not the only available solution to the stereo problem; another algorithm of note, named *PMF* from the initials of its inventors, has been developed at the University of Sheffield (Pollard et al., 1985) and is now an integral part of a commercially available system (Porril et al., 1987) for industrial object identification and location.[*]

A Stereo Algorithm

A simple camera model will be used to illustrate the operation of stereo. Remember from Chapter 3 that the world is focussed by a lens onto some sort of target. Regarding the target as the *image plane*, we use the model shown in Figure 8.2; the obvious analogy is the eye focussing an image onto the retina. The distance from the image plane to the lens is f.

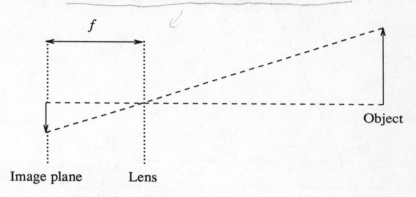

Object

Image plane   Lens

Figure 8.2 A simple camera model

A simple diagram demonstrates how we might use a two camera system to determine the depth (distance from viewer(s)) of image points. In Figure 8.3, which is purely schematic, we have a bird's eye view of two cameras separated by a distance $2h$ and the images they provide, together with one point P with co-ordinates (x,y,z) in the scene, showing this point's projection onto left (P_l) and right (P_r) images. The co-ordinates in this Figure have the z axis representing distance from the cameras (at which $z=0$) and the x axis representing "horizontal" distance (the y co-ordinate, into the page, does not therefore appear). $x=0$ will be the position midway between the cameras; each image will have a local co-ordinate system (x_l on the left, x_r on the right), which for the sake of convenience we measure from the centre of the respective images; that is, a simple translation from the global x co-ordinate. Without fear of confusion we use P_l simultaneously to represent the position of the projection of P onto the left image, and its x_l co-ordinate - its distance from the centre of the left image (and similarly for

---

[*]TINA: details on this system are available from the Artificial Intelligence and Vision Research Unit, University of Sheffield, Sheffield, S10 2TN, UK.

P_r).

It is clear that there is a *disparity* between x_l and x_r as a result of the different camera positions (that is, $|P_l-P_r|>0$); we can use elementary geometry to deduce the z co-ordinate of P.

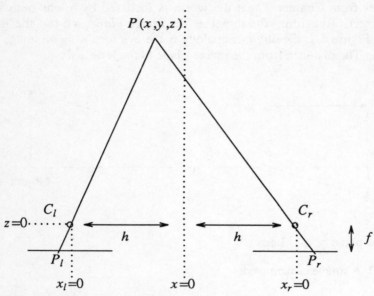

Figure 8.3 Elementary stereo geometry

We notice that P_l, C_l and C_l, P are the hypotenuses of similar right-angled triangles. Noting that h and f are (positive) numbers, z is a positive co-ordinate and x, P_l, P_r are co-ordinates that may be positive or negative, we can then write:

$$\frac{P_l}{f} = -\frac{(h+x)}{z}$$

and similarly from the right of Figure 8.3

$$\frac{P_r}{f} = \frac{(h-x)}{z}$$

Eliminating x from these equations gives

$$z(P_r-P_l) = 2hf$$

and hence

$$z = \frac{2hf}{P_r - P_l}$$

Notice in this equation that $P_r - P_l$ is the detected disparity in the observations of P. If $P_r - P_l = 0$ then $z = \infty$ - quite correctly we observe that no disparity indicates the point is (effectively) at an infinite distance from the viewer.

It all seems very easy: Find the points, match them and then an elementary calculation yields three dimensional co-ordinates. In fact, of course, this begs some very serious questions. Which points are matched, and how? Given a set of "features" from one image - probably edges or corners detected in some obvious way by searching for sharp intensity changes - how do we derive the stereo correspondence when there is no guarantee even (without further information) that a point in one image appears at all in the other? This is the stereo correspondence problem.

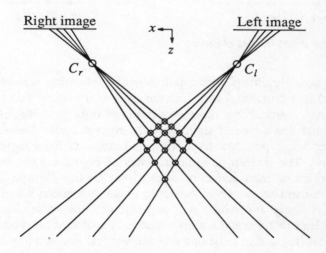

Figure 8.4 Stereo projections of four points

One early, successful and well known solution to this problem will now be described (Marr & Poggio, 1979). The presentation in the original reference is very clear, and accordingly we follow it quite closely here. Assuming that we have an array of points to match from both images (where these points may of course represent edges or boundaries, but may just as well represent "corners"), we can apply two intuitively obvious constraints;

(1)   A given point has a unique position in space. Therefore each feature provides at most one disparity value by matching exactly one point in

the other image.

(2) Matter is cohesive, and surfaces are smooth compared with their distance from the observer. We may therefore deduce that disparity is continuous almost everywhere.

To illustrate the algorithm, consider the problem in one dimension only - four colinear points are viewed by two cameras C_r and C_l; this is shown schematically in Figure 8.4. Each image contains four points (L_1, L_2, L_3, L_4 and R_1, R_2, R_3, R_4) - see Figure 8.5. The correct "matching" is to pair L_i with R_i for $i=1,2,3,4$, but we cannot know this automatically. Each line intersection in Figure 8.4 represents a possible match of points in the left and right images; we require to filter out the incorrect matches and leave four mutually consistent matches (indicated by the filled circles).

Figure 8.5 The stereo images observed

Consider now "plotting" these points in the following manner; the left image is used as a horizontal axis, and the right as a vertical axis (as in Figure 8.6). Here, a vertical line represents a line of sight from the left camera, and a horizontal line a line of sight from the right camera. Intersections of these lines represent possible disparities, and diagonal lines represent constant disparity. The sixteen possible matches of Figure 8.4 are represented by sixteen points of intersection of dotted lines on this "graph". We can now use the constraints observed earlier to make deductions about which of these points is likely and which not; in particular, the constraint that each feature provides exactly one disparity value tells us that at most one point on each horizontal line and at most one on each vertical line is a true match. At initialisation each such line will have many putative points, so we need an algorithm that discards all but one. Secondly, the smoothness constraint says that disparity should not vary "too fast" - therefore points close on this graph are likely to lie on the diagonal lines.

These two observations suggest a relaxation scheme in which the initial state is all the points being equally likely, but their likelihoods being refined by using the diagonal lines to reinforce and the vertical and horizontal lines to inhibit. The approach is to imagine the grid generated as Figure 8.6 as a network of processors, with a 1 loaded wherever two dots may match (at each intersection). Iteratively, vertical and horizontal neighbours will now inhibit each other while diagonal neighbours reinforce; *inhibitory* and

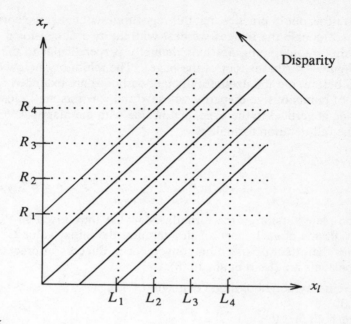

Figure 8.6

excitatory neighbourhoods will be defined to control this influence. We hope that such a scheme converges in the sense that there will eventually be at most one 1 on each row and column, representing the correct match.

More formally, we may try the following iterative scheme. Without loss of generality, we consider the left image - remembering that currently our image is in one dimension only, for a given x_l co-ordinate we are interested in its most likely "disparity co-ordinate" d; for convenience in what follows, write $x=x_l$. Define $C^n_{x,d}$ to be the contents of the processor representing co-ordinate x and disparity d at the nth iteration. Iteration 0 will initialise $C^0_{x,d}$ with all the possible matches; we can then write

$$C^{(n+1)}_{x,d} = \sigma(\sum_{x',d' \varepsilon S(x,d)} C^n_{x',d'} - \sum_{x',d' \varepsilon O(x,d)} C^n_{x',d'})$$

where $S(x,d)$ is the excitatory neighbourhood of (x,d) and $O(x,d)$ is the inhibitory neighbourhood. σ is a simple threshold function which sets the new value of the processor to 0 or 1 dependent on the magnitude of the bracketed expression.

If the neighbourhoods are defined "sensibly" (in particular, of course, they should contain the point (x,d)) then it should be clear that a solution to the matching problem is a fixed point of the iteration, while unstable points are not. It turns out in practice that this algorithm will converge correctly.

In fact of course the images we deal with are two dimensional - we can cater for this by imagining a y axis mutually perpendicular to the x and z axes of Figure 8.4 (that is, out of the page). The inhibitory neighbourhoods remain as before, but the excitatory neighbourhoods are extended to include a "disc" of points of like disparity whose x and y points are "close". This disc's plane is vertical to the page, and in line with the diagonal "excitatory line". The full iteration formula is;

$$C^{(n+1)}_{x,y,d} = \qquad\qquad\qquad\qquad\qquad\qquad\qquad\qquad 8.1$$

$$\sigma(\sum_{x',y',d' \epsilon S(x,y,d)} C^n_{x',y',d'} - \theta \sum_{x',y',d' \epsilon O(x,y,d)} C^n_{x',y',d'} + C^0_{x,y,d})$$

In this complete version of the formula, Marr has introduced an "inhibition constant" θ, and at each stage of the iteration the initial value C^0 is added in; this has the effect of speeding convergence. Successful practical values for the constants are (Marr et al., 1978):

an excitatory neighbourhood diameter of 5.0;
$\theta=2.0$;
a threshold of 3.0.

This algorithm is not by any means the only approach to the stereo problem - indeed it is one of the earlier ones and has been simplified for presentation here (for instance, the function σ may in practice not be a simple threshold). The interested reader is referred to the University of Sheffield work (Pollard et al., 1985).

Depth Map Technologies

The "Shape from ..." ideas can be thought of as *passive* range finding techniques in the sense that nothing is actually projected onto the scene. Other such passive schemes exist - we may for instance "sense" depth by determining the necessary focus of wide aperture lenses, whose depth of field is very small.

Alternatively, we may consider *active* depth sensing where the detection of object distance from the sensor is a primary rather than secondary aim, and is achieved by projection (probably of some electromagnetic wave) onto the scene. Such schemes appear to us as special purpose in the sense that we are not accustomed to doing this ourselves (other animals such of bats make heavy use of such ideas, of course). Active depth sensors will produce pixel arrays where the pixel values encode the depth from the sensor of that point of the scene - the price we pay is a loss of all the intensity information. It may be argued that this is a very heavy price; even in the complete absence of depth data the multitude of clues provided by intensity data gives a great deal of information.

The predominant technology for active depth sensing is lasers. Sometimes called ''spot ranging'', this technique involves beaming a laser spot at the scene and measuring the reflection; depth may actually be determined by timing the delay in the return or measuring the phase difference between the reflection and the original. The former technique can provide good quality data but requires electronics with a very fine resolution (of the order of 70 picoseconds to determine depth to a precision of 0.005m). It may also, for high quality results, demand a laser of such power as to be harmful to human beings. The latter technique is, in relative terms, slow, perhaps requiring minutes to capture one image of a scene (Jarvis 1983).

We can remark in passing that spot range data is susceptible to many of the segmentation techniques we have developed for intensity images; Hough transforms, region growers and simple edge detectors will work as well on depth data as they do on grey level matrices.

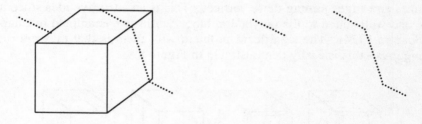

Figure 8.7 A light stripe, and the output presented

An older active depth sensing technique, which is intuitively more simple, is *light striping*. Here we site a camera at a known (x,y,z) co-ordinate, and shine a stripe of light along a plane, also of known co-ordinates. We will see a single stripe of light in the scene - we may actually do this by shining the light in a darkened room or by using a laser source that will be detectable anyway. Given that the plane and camera co-ordinates are known, provided the focal point of the camera does not lie in the plane of the light, simple co-ordinate geometry permits the depth of any object intersecting the light stripe to be determined - Figure 8.7 illustrates the principle of the idea. Comprehensive depth information is extracted by shining a (probably parallel) selection of stripes at the scene. This idea has defects in that, unless the stripe directions are carefully chosen, concavities in the scene will not appear at all, and that surfaces near parallel to the range of stripes will provide relatively little data since they will intersect few stripes. On the other hand, the continuous lines the stripes present on a given surface allow simple and accurate segmentation of light stripe data, in contrast to spot range data.

Modelling the World

Hitherto we have said nothing about how, once information has been extracted from an image or images, real world objects are identified. We need to construct a *model* of the objects in view. This glibly stated problem is in fact difficult, large and far from solved. It would be easy to produce many books under the title ''Model Based Vision'', but this volume is purely introductory, and here we will restrict ourselves to an overview of some of the better known techniques.

Wire Frames

A very well known and elementary way of representing solids is as a list of vertices and edges joining those vertices. This is an attractive idea since it is fast, and well suited to the polyhedral block worlds we examined in Chapter 7 (Shapira 1974). The significant problem with them is that they are often ambiguous - this is easily demonstrated in Figure 8.8.

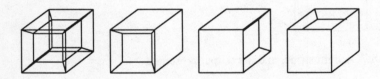

Figure 8.8 Wire frame ambiguity

Constructive Solid Geometry (CSG)

A relatively recent idea which has found some success, notably with IBM's WINSOM (Morris & Quarendon, 1985) and the University of Leeds Geometric Modelling Project's NONAME (Armstrong et al., 1982), is to construct 3D bodies from a selection of *primitives*. Popularly, these primitives are a block, a cylinder a sphere and a cone - they are scaled, positioned and combined by union, intersection and difference. The versatility of such a simply stated scheme is surprising. In contrast to wire frames, CSG models define properties such as object volume unambiguously, but suffer the drawback of being non-unique. That is, a body may have several equally valid CSG representations; further, it is not easy to model "natural" shapes (a head, for instance) with CSG. A more serious drawback is that it is not straightforward to recover *surfaces* given a CSG description; such a procedure is very computationally expensive.

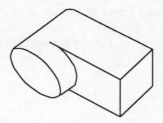

Figure 8.9 A boundary representation problem

Boundary Representations

Boundary representations, often referred to as *B-reps*, are an appealing and intuitively natural way of representing 3D bodies in that they consist of an explicit list of the bodies' faces. "Faces" are usually taken to be planar, so bodies are always polyhedral, and we are dealing the whole time with piecewise planar surfaces. A useful side effect of this scheme is that properties such as surface area and solid volume are well defined. The simplest B-rep scheme would model everything with the simplest possible 2D polygon, the triangle; by taking small enough primitives quite satisfactory representations of complex objects can be achieved, and it is an obvious generalisation to consider polygons with more edges than three.

A drawback with these B-reps is that "face" may not be well defined. We would hope that a face should have no "dangling" edges, and that the union of a body's faces should be its boundary. Unfortunately the real world is not co-operative and many (simple) bodies exist in which face boundaries are not well defined - Figure 8.9 provides just one example.

Another generalisation of the scheme is to permit the faces to be defined by spline based surfaces; this permits much greater flexibility in the description, but it becomes important to restrict the number of possible face edges in order to limit the complexity of the computations involved.

Generalised Cones

Recall that a cylinder may be defined as the surface swept out by a circle whose centre is travelling along a straight line normal to the circle's plane (see Figure 8.10). We can generalise this idea in a number of ways - we may permit any closed curve to be "pulled along" any line in three space. We may even permit the closed curve to adjust as it travels in accordance with some function, so a cone is defined by a circle whose radius changes linearly with distance travelled, moving along a straight line.

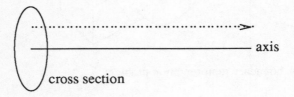

cross section

Figure 8.10 The generalised cone principle

These generalised cones (sometimes called *generalised cylinders*), specified by a spine, cross section and sweeping rule, turn out to be very good at representing some classes of solid body (Binford 1971, Soroka & Bajcsy, 1978). Remember that the closed curve may be, for instance, a polygon, permitting bodies with straight edges to be generated very easily. A well known Vision system called ACRONYM (Brooks et al., 1979) uses generalised cones as its modelling scheme - ACRONYM is discussed further in the next two Chapters.

There can be problems modelling "natural" bodies, for example the human form, with generalised cones; while the limbs and torso lend themselves well to the scheme, heads do not. Likewise, landscapes do not lend themselves to the idea. Industrial components on the other hand may very well be assembled from generalised cone primitives.

It is common for users of generalised cones to restrict the closed curves they admit to be circles.

These listed representation schemes are not all that is available; other ideas such as oct-trees (Meagher 1981) or skeleton representations (Garibotto & Tosini, 1982) are equally valid. It is worth bearing in mind that 3D representations may be developed with one of three aims in mind; the first is what we want - an aid to recognising 3D structures from 2D, 2.5D (Marr 1982) or 3D information gleaned from images. The second is the graphics aim of displaying pictures of modelled objects, with all the problems of rendering etc. that this implies. A third aim would be in CAD systems, where physical properties of solids (inertia, mass etc.) need to be quickly accessible from the model. These aims have different requirements and this means that schemes suitable for one may not be suitable for the others. In particular, wire frames and CSG are good tools for 3D display systems, while boundary representations are perhaps more suitable for the recognition/matching task. It has been observed (Besl & Jain, 1985) that it will be necessary to evaluate surfaces somewhere in a Vision system since range data consists of sampled surface data, while intensity images depend strongly on object surface geometry.

For a full and authoritative account of 3D representations, see (Requicha 1980) and (Requicha & Voelcker, 1982).

Remarks

We have established in this Chapter that 3D information may be acquired about the real world by a variety of means, and demonstrated one algorithm for so doing. This represents the culmination of the process of extracting information from the image or images, howsoever they were acquired, and is followed by the process of matching what is seen to what is known about the "world model". That we have come this far should not be taken as an indication that this phase of the Vision process is a solved problem,. or that necessarily there is agreement on how the problem *should* be solved. Following on from "information extraction" of course comes the whole new problem of "matching" - it is at this time that Artificial Intelligence techniques come to bear, and the remainder of the book is devoted to them.

Some remarks on what we have achieved to date are relevant. With the assistance of a couple of leaps of faith (for example, reliable noise extraction, accurate segmentation and enough information to drive some form of Shape from ... algorithm), it can be acknowledged that starting from "images" it is usually possible to move to a 3D representation of that which is visible. We may observe that exhaustive 3D co-ordinate information is probably going to be neither necessary nor desirable. Conceptually, the Vision task is the inverse of the 3D graphics task in that starting with a "picture" we wish to recognise what is in it, while graphics involves taking a known object co-ordinate list and generating a (2D) representation. The latter task certainly needs exhaustive information about the objects and their locations (and for full representations, their colour and the lighting properties), and many graphics books are devoted to it (Foley & Van Dam, 1982, Newman & Sproull, 1979). On the other hand, it may well be possible to identify objects in an image from a reduced set of information; provided the "alphabet" of that which is likely to be in the scene is well known, it will be sufficient to identify a characteristic feature of each object. This will have important consequences for the amount of information that we carry around, and for how soon a "match" will be determined. For example, if we are looking at a picture of a bicycle it is enough to identify two wheels, handlebars, saddle and pedals - it will (probably) not be necessary to identify each spoke of the wheels, or to count the sprockets on the gearing. This is certainly not a part of the human's recognition of a bicycle.

We might also remark that the requirement for 3D information has yet to be demonstrated, and that the Vision problem may be soluble from just 2D information (that is, a *3D* Vision problem - we are not talking here about the pure 2D problems such as character recognition and PCB analysis). Obviously, human beings can recognise representations of 3D objects when the evidence is genuinely 2D - we can identify a bicycle just as well from a photograph as from the real thing; there is no need to perform stereopsis or analyze motion since our brain's model of the real world has enough information on the basis of pure 2D clues. Vision systems that operate solely on the basis of 2D analysis have been constructed; one of these (Goad 1983) uses a 3D model of a simple object to interpret what it sees and is outlined in Appendix IV as an example. Another, relatively recent, approach (Lowe 1985) suggests that "perceptual organisation" is enough for accurate recognition. That is, clues such as long continuous boundaries, with properties such as parallelism of lines or concentricity of circles, may be enough to complete identification - the task is to isolate "rules" that discriminate well. Vision systems built on such principles by-pass the difficult stages that have only been outlined in this Chapter, since they make depth data redundant. It is not suggested, though, that such solutions are better or worse than depth map based ideas - this area of Computer Vision is very fertile for research efforts.

Exercises

(1)   [Optical flow] If we are presented with a series of images changing "smoothly" with time, suppose we represent the intensity at point (x,y) and time t by $f(x,y,t)$. We may expect the image at time $t+\delta t$ to be a translation of the image at time t by δx and δy, so

$$f(x+\delta x, y+\delta y, t+\delta t) = f(x,y,t)$$

Expand the expression on the left hand side of this equation as a Taylor series, and truncate it at the first term, thereby deriving an equation relating $\dfrac{dx}{dt}$ and $\dfrac{dy}{dt}$ with quantities measurable from the image

sequence.
(2) Why, when light striping, should we keep the focal point of the camera out of the light plane?
(3) There is a second possible interpretation of Figure 8.4; that is, the images of Figure 8.5 may arise from a different arrangement of points than that shown in Figure 8.4. What is it, and why would it not be found by the Marr Poggio algorithm?
(4) Consider Equation 8.1 together with the values of constants quoted in the text. What does the algorithm do with completely isolated points, in whose excitatory neighbourhood no other points fall?

CHAPTER 9

Knowledge Representation

Introduction

Hitherto we have not considered how to describe collections of different objects in a scene. There are a number of Artificial Intelligence formalisms available for this purpose, for example, predicate calculus (logic), production systems, and semantic networks (Levesque 1986).

Logic is formal, with well defined semantics. However it is not always a very "natural" tool for scene descriptions. Production systems are flexible, but lack structure: they will be studied in detail in the next chapter. Semantic networks are intuitively appealing but usually lack a formal semantic basis so that it is not always easy to predict the various side-effects of computations; nevertheless this shortcoming has not mattered for small, experimental systems built to pursue limited objectives.

 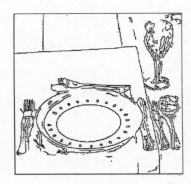

Figure 9.1 A place setting, and its edges

The advantages of a formal, high level, well behaved knowledge representation system are that it is possible to describe very rich scenes and also make useful deductions about it. In principle it should be possible to deduce what some partially visible object might be if there exists a model of what it looks like. For example if we know that houses generally have back and front doors, we would find it easy to deduce that a particular region in an image is probably a path to the back door even if we can only see part of the front. In practice this type of common sense reasoning is very hard to build. The examples in this and the next chapter should help to illustrate this.

Thus the approach taken in these two chapters is to base the discussion on pragmatic approaches though they may lack the formal rigour of earlier low level techniques.

Semantic Networks and Frames

Semantic networks have been used and developed by many Artificial Intelligence workers. In this section we tend towards a formal type of semantic network based on Nilsson's (Nilsson 1982) description of binary predicate calculus and its graphical representation.

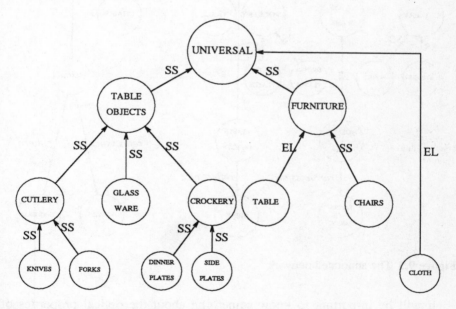

Figure 9.2 A semantic network for the dinner table

The network is a directed graph of nodes and arcs in which each arc connects exactly two nodes. Nodes represent CONSTANTS or *variables*, while arcs show the predicates EL (element of) or SS (subset of) or else a unary *function*.

Thus in the dinner table example from Chapter 1, we could have nodes to represent: the sets of furniture, cutlery, glassware, crockery, the table, the table cloth, etc; by convention there is also a root node, UNIVERSAL. The use of EL and SS arcs should be self evident as in Figure 9.2.

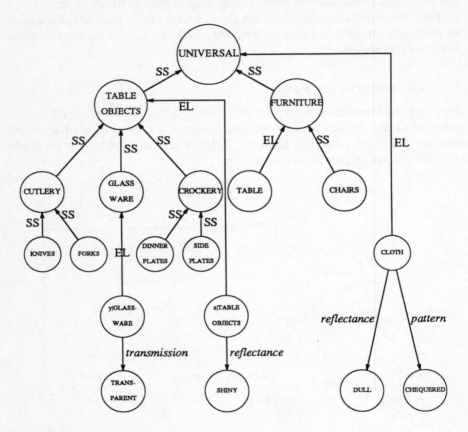

Figure 9.3 The annotated network

It will be important to know something about the optical properties of these objects, for example that the cloth has a chequered pattern, or that the glassware is transparent, or that cutlery, crockery and glassware shine. The net can easily be annotated to show these, although the provision of corresponding low-level processing techniques need not concern us here. In the case of the table cloth, we wish to describe the property of a single element in the network: accordingly an arc labelled with the function *pattern* is directed from CLOTH to a node called CHEQUERED. When a property of a whole set of objects is to be described, the situation is slightly more complicated. First of all a special element of the set is created, called a delineation node represented here by x|TABLE OBJECTS meaning that x is a global variable of sort TABLE OBJECTS. Then the property is added with a function arc as before. All the descendant nodes of TABLE OBJECTS inherit its properties; any exceptions to the defaults can be explicitly added to appropriate nodes. The result is a network as shown in Figure 9.3. Note that it says nothing about the reflectance or pattern of the furniture.

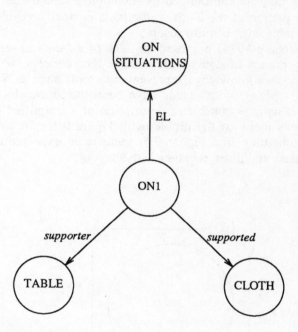

Figure 9.4 The ON relation

The next requirement of the evolving model is to describe some important spatial relationships. The method used here is influenced by the work of Winston (Winston 1975) which will be considered in more detail later. For example CLOTH is ''on'' the table and TABLE OBJECTS are ''on'' CLOTH. One form of representation would simply be to think of ''on'' as a property of an object; the problem with this is that it is not very general and provides rather poor potential access for reasoning purposes. A far better approach is to set up a node to represent the set of ON relations, for each of which there is a *supporter* subject and a *supported* object. Figure 9.4 demonstrates this for a subset of the total network using TABLE and

CLOTH. The power of this structure becomes clearer when more complicated relations such as top-middle-bottom are considered. Also there is no reason why the different nodes cannot be added as information becomes available: a more compact structure might not allow this.

Very often when reasoning about a scene, there will be stereotypical situations. In our domain, for example, there is a recurring group of objects which make up a place setting - we see how these may be detected in Figure 9.1. Notice in passing that attempts at unambiguous identification of cutlery and plate here may be confounded by incomplete boundaries. Notice also that while the pattern of the cloth *on* the table is clearly visible in the edge detection, the table edge is quite absent!

Minsky (Minsky 1975) proposed the idea of a *frame* to represent naturally occurring groups of domain knowledge. His concept has been widely taken up in modern knowledge representation tools such as KEE (Fikes & Kehler, 1985). Many of the ideas have been introduced by our notation already, but let us now consider a description of a simplified place setting, which overlooks many of the problems in Figure 9.1. An ideal plan view might look something like Figure 9.5; there is an expectation of a knife, fork, spoon, glass and plate, together with a layout.

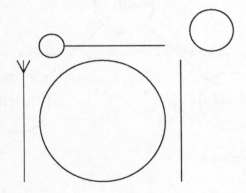

Figure 9.5 A place setting

There will be a set of PLACE SETTINGS each element of which has *slots* for spoons, forks and so on. In Figure 9.6 the slots point to *fillers*, such as the single element fork, but they could have pointed to a more complicated structure to represent, say, a variable number of forks of different types. Thus a simple hierarchy provides a flexible representation of a place setting. In passing we note that here the definition of the slot functions, for example *left*, can be at a lower level of processing than the knowledge representation system and could be implemented via function calls.

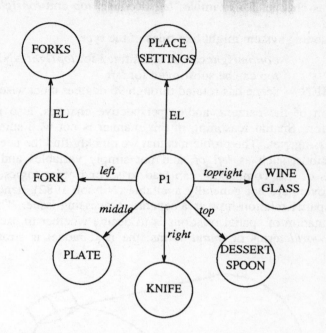

Figure 9.6 A place setting frame

Reasoning about Spatial Relationships

Careful consideration of the structures presented will leave the reader with an understanding for the complexity of Computer Vision systems. For example, Figure 9.7 taken from Winston (Winston 1975) indicates the difficulty in deciding just what ''left-of'' means.

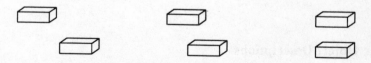

Figure 9.7 When is the upper block ''left''?

There is a more serious difficulty though. The PLACE SETTING frame included location data defined from a particular perspective: a plan viewed from the bottom of Figure 9.5. Viewed from the right hand side of the plan, the functions change, for example: *left* becomes *top* and *topright* becomes *bottomright*.

Our reasoning system might like rules of the type

IF   *bottomright* can be substituted for *topright* **AND**
              top can be substituted for *left*
THEN   scene has rotated through 90 degrees clockwise.

The location of the camera, and/or perspective changes, also need to be accounted for. Spatial reasoning in this manner is not well suited to symbolic processing, yet. The problem is that we quickly find the need to reason about functions, such as *left_of*, and not simply variables and constants. Expressions of this complexity can lead to second order logics, for which theorem provers are not generally available (Nilsson 1982), hence the need to handle spatial relationships as a separate processing issue. The key idea for representation of spatial relations is to decide whether to use models of objects in *world* terms or *image* terms; the next model is strongly world oriented.

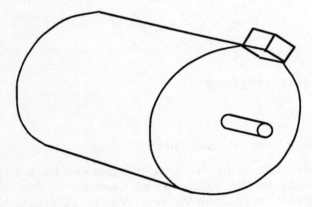

Figure 9.8 A generalised cone motor with shaft and one flange

Generic Object Descriptions

The frame concept has been adopted for the ACRONYM model based vision system (Brooks et al., 1979). There is also extensive use of generalised cones, introduced in Chapter 8, and production systems to be dealt with in the next Chapter. The use of *geometric reasoning* to handle spatial relationships is also important. In the present discussion we are interested in the representation of objects in a hierarchical fashion starting with coarse detail and working down to more fine detail. The objects are frames in an object graph (Brooks 1983).

Recall that a generalised cone is defined by a spine, a cross section and a sweeping rule. A simple electric motor, with one flange, is shown in Figure 9.8. We could define a specific electric motor as a frame:

```
Node: ELECTRIC_MOTOR
   CLASS:              SIMPLE_CONE
   SPINE:              STRAIGHT_LENGTH_8
   SWEEPING_RULE:      CONSTANT
   CROSS_SECTION:      CIRCLE_RADIUS_2.5
```

So far so good, but it would obviously be useful to represent the fillers of slots by frames themselves, as indicated below. Before looking at that, we generalise it to produce a *generic* description of a motor. At this stage let us purely confine the discussion to the dimensions. Instead of a constant as a slot filler, we can optionally use inequalities. So the motor length could be anything between 6.0 and 9.0 units long and the radius could vary:

$$6.0 \leq MOTOR\_LENGTH \leq 9.0$$
$$2.0 \leq MOTOR\_RADIUS \leq 3.0$$

These *quantifiers* are actually held in a separate structure called the *restriction graph*. A generic electric motor body model (Brooks 1981) will look as follows:

```
Node: GENERIC_ELECTRIC_MOTOR_CONE
   CLASS:              SIMPLE_CONE
   SPINE:              Z0014
   SWEEPING_RULE:      CONSTANT_SWEEPING_RULE
   CROSS_SECTION:      Z0013

Node: Z00014
   CLASS:     SPINE
   TYPE:      STRAIGHT
   LENGTH:    MOTOR_LENGTH

Node: CONSTANT_SWEEPING_RULE
   CLASS:     SWEEPING RULE
   TYPE:      CONSTANT

Node: Z0013
   CLASS:     CROSS_SECTION
   TYPE:      CIRCLE
```

RADIUS: MOTOR_RADIUS

We have now described the object frames of the object graph; arcs are actually frames of classes called *sub-part* and *affixment*. Suppose our motor body has flanges, then a flange can be described in object frames similar to the ones for the motor body. In the sub-part frames there will be slots for the quantity of flanges on a motor and the reference to the flange frame itself. The filler for the quantity can be an inequality constraint, so that a family of motors with different numbers of flanges can be described. The affixment frames are used to hold the geometric transformation between the motor body and one flange. Recall that each object frame is modelled in its own local co-ordinate system. Therefore a combination of a rotation and translation is required to bring two local systems together. The affixment frame also has a quantity slot to shown the transformation required between each sub-part when there is more than one. For example four flanges would be rotated 90 degrees each.

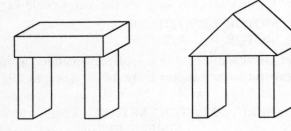

Figure 9.9 Some ''correct'' arches

Winston's Arch

For completeness we mention here an example of a semantic network which is often quoted. It concerns the structural description of an arch. The importance of the work is that the semantic network was learnt by a program devised by Winston (Winston 1970, Winston 1975, Winston 1984). The system was given an example of an arch, and then several more examples and counter-examples (near-misses), as shown in Figures 9.9 and 9.10. From each image it would learn that an arc in the network MUST exist, MUST_NOT exist, or other possibilities. It would learn that an arch consists of a brick or wedge supported by two bricks which must not touch. The work shows how difficult it is to learn explicit knowledge and does not have the flexibility of WISARD (Chapter 2), but it does have a little depth.

In the long term the best chance of progress in the area of learning may come from research into Connectionist Machines, which consist of a richly interconnected network of tiny, McCulloch Pitts type, processors. During their learning phase, the strength of the interconnections is determined by reference to a teaching set (Rumelhart & McClelland 1986).

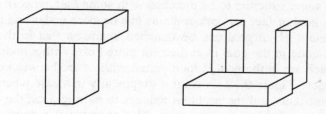

Figure 9.10 Some "near-miss" arches

Syntactic Descriptions

An alternative approach to semantic networks is to describe the syntax of a scene in terms of small primitive elements which can be combined together according to rules specified in a grammar. Consider the trivial example of the "staircase" structure in Figure 9.11. The primitives could be lines of unit length in the horizontal and vertical directions, denoted by *h* and *v* respectively. Appropriate parsing techniques, perhaps using some of the production system techniques outlined in Chapter 10, might generate *hhvhvhvh* as a description of the staircase. Low level processing, such as the Hough transforms in Chapter 5 could identify the primitives in the image.

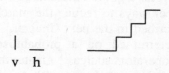

v h

Figure 9.11 A staircase and its primitives

At one stage in the history of Computer Vision, there were attempts to model 3D objects in syntax. A very short, readable introduction to the ideas is available in Duda and Hart (Duda 1973). For limited domains such as the classification of fingerprints or chromosomes, syntax based methods do work well. Extensive treatments are available elsewhere (Gonzalez &

Thomason, 1978, Miclet 1986).

Matching

A common problem in Vision is to try to *match* some structure in the processed image with a corresponding part of a semantic network. Let the *goal network* be some structure to be matched with some *fact network* in the database. Each goal or fact network contains one or more nodes and arcs. In the simplest case a given goal can be matched against a fact in the following way: every node in the goal is unified (or paired off) with a node in the fact network; each arc in the goal is then paired with an arc between corresponding fact nodes. Figure 9.12 shows this graphically in a case where the nodes represent constants and the problem reduces to pairing arcs; the ones which dip below the dotted line are goal arcs. This example also demonstrates that a goal network may match a subnetwork of the fact; it is clearly semantically reasonable to match a network of salt and pepper with a cruet set even though no mustard is present. Had the goal and fact networks been the other way around, there would have been no match. This indicates why a matching process may well work from the general to the particular, as in ACRONYM (Brooks 1983). We could start by trying to match electric motor bodies, then move onto the flanges, and so on until a specific instance was identified.

There is a problem for the designer of Computer Vision systems when considering the level of domain dependent structure to put in the representation system. The more structure there is, the quicker the matching, but generality is lost. In simple cases the matching process can often be reduced to finding isomorphisms between graphs. This process is computationally intense: in general it is NP. The complexity can be reduced, however, if we can make sensible guesses about which substructures are the most important in matching. Simon provides a good treatment of the issues (Simon 1986).

Finally, there are other ways to reduce the matching problem which are used in the systems described in the next Chapter. For instance, the degree of match could be determined on a probabilistic basis (Ohta et al., 1979, Shapiro 1983), or operators such as "greater than" could work on properties like length or area (Nazif & Levine, 1984, Adorni et al., 1985). Once again it can be seen that numerical processing may have advantages over symbolic processing in Vision (Ambler 1975).

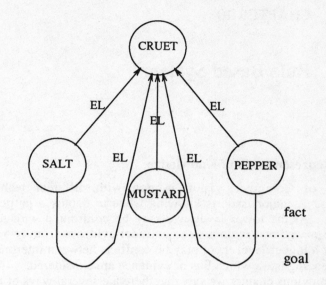

Figure 9.12 Matching goals and facts

Exercises

(1) Use the ACRONYM generalised cone and frame approach to create single frames to represent
    (i) a dinner plate
    (ii) a piece of generic cutlery
    (iii) the table top in two different ways.
You will need to be fairly relaxed and imaginative in the simplifications you adopt.
(2) Briefly consider some problems in the representation of a fork at a level of detail which indicates the different prongs.
(3) Examine Figure 1.9 to see which parts of letters may match each other erroneously.

CHAPTER 10

Rule Based Systems

Explicit Representation of Knowledge

The field of Computer Vision is rich with different techniques and approaches. A major issue is knowing when to deploy a particular line of processing. At the lower levels we may be confronted with decisions on whether to merge two regions or to consider evidence from two boundaries, whereas at a higher level there may be conflicts between interpretations of a scene depending upon which bits of evidence are considered.

In the previous chapter we saw that there are several ways of representing knowledge, each with advantages and disadvantages. It has been expedient in several Vision systems now extant to use *rule based* systems to satisfy the diverse needs of representational power and processing efficiency. They also provide a flexible method to encode ad-hoc rules of thumb.

Rule based systems can be conceptualised as *production systems* which are overviewed in the following section. After that various practical examples are given to demonstrate the power of the rule based approach in Vision.

Overview of Production Systems

Production systems are widely employed in Computer Science and Artificial Intelligence. They can be employed to process syntactic definitions of languages (Aho 1986), or as the basis of an expert system (Waterman 1986) or (Jackson 1986).

The basic components of a production system are: a set of *rules*, a *database*, and an *interpreter* (sometimes called a control system) (Davis and King, 1977). The rules are of the form:

IF condition **THEN** action

The *condition side*, also called the *left hand side*, consists of a set of conditions whose truth can be evaluated by reference to the contents of the database. The *action side*, or *right hand side*, corresponds to a set of actions which are performed on the database.

Associated with the database are its initial state and some set of goal states. The interpreter can operate in a forwards or backwards direction. Let us first consider forwards, or *pattern directed*, behaviour. The interpreter scans down the left hand side of the rule set and each set of conditions is evaluated to see if it is currently true or false. A (possibly empty) subset of the rule set will evaluate as true: this is called the conflict set. One rule is taken from the conflict set and fired, that is the action side is executed to change the state of the database; the cycle is then repeated. For obvious reasons the process is sometimes called the recognise-act cycle. The process continues until a goal state is reached in the database. Backward chaining is essentially the reverse of this.

The overall behaviour can best be illustrated with a very simple example. Consider the following production:

(i)	d	&	a	==>	b
(ii)	a	&	f	==>	e
(iii)	a	&	c	==>	d
(iv)	b	&	d	==>	f

Suppose we are given that a and c are true. Is e true? For the sake of simplicity, let our conflict resolution strategy be to take first the rule with the lowest number which has not already fired. Proceeding by forward chaining we first evaluate the left-hand sides.
(1)   Only (iii) is true, so it fires adding $d=true$ to the database.
(2)   Now our conflict set contains (i) and (iii). Thus (i) fires, and $b=true$ is added to the database.
(3)   Now (i), (iii) and (iv) are true, so we take (iv); thus f is now true.
(4)   Finally all the rules are in the conflict set, so (ii) fires, proving that e is true.

In backward chaining, or *goal-directed* behaviour, the reasoning proceeds as follows:
(1)   Rule (ii) would give us what we want if a and f were known to be true. Recursively set up subgoals to prove a and f true. We know a a *priori*, so find out if f is true.
(2)   To satisfy the subgoal for f, select rule (iv). Recursively set up subgoals to prove the truth of b and d. For b we select (i); a is known *a priori*; so prove d to be true.
(3)   To prove the truth of d, select (iii). a and c are both known *a priori*; therefore d is true; therefore b is true; therefore f is true.
(4)   Therefore we know e is true by rule (ii).

One thing should be made very clear at this stage. It is that the control strategy is crucial to the efficiency of the system. The proof procedure can be thought of as graph-walking. At one extreme we can adopt a breadth-first strategy, at the other a depth-first one. There are trade-offs between the certainty of finding a solution, and the optimality of the path to the solution (Nilsson 1982).

Segmentation

In this section we examine certain features of a rule based approach to segmentation (Nazif & Levine, 1984). Here our usual image is stored in the database; the actions of rules correspond to low level operators, for instance region merge; and the interpreter, as we shall see, is fundamentally forward chaining. An important concept in this system is an *area* which is a contiguous, usually non-overlapping partition of the image derived from factors such as texture rather than mere co-ordinates; the system concentrates, or *focuses it attention*, on one area at a time.

It will be apparent from earlier Chapters that there are many possible ways in which an image can be segmented. For example should emphasis be placed on boundary analysis or region growing, or within segmentation should priority at some particular stage be given to splitting regions or merging others? The idea behind the current work is to control such possible low-level operations within a production system. The structure of the system is given in Figure 10.1.

From a production systems point of view, an unusual feature is the way control is managed: this will be discussed over the next few paragraphs. The database is called the short term memory, and the rules are stored in the long term memory. Control resides in any one of the processes at a particular instant, but the decision on which process to invoke is taken using the focus of attention rules and meta rules. The processes themselves more or less correspond to the action part of rules; for example functions in the line analysis process include *extend line forward*, *delete line* and *join lines backward*.

The short term memory contains the initial image and data on the current sets of regions and lines (in the cited authors' terminology for this system a *line* corresponds to what we have hitherto called boundaries; it is part of the boundary of some region). For each image pixel, labels indicate the region it is in and the line it is on, if any. For each region there is also data on its average colour, position and so on, and in addition lines can be marked as parallel etc. When processing terminates the segmentation data is available in short term memory. An internal control requirement is to create and store areas for focusing attention so that the system can be directed to work intensely on a small area of the image.

The rules in the long term memory are grouped according to function. The *line*, *region* and *area rule sets* are associated with actions in their

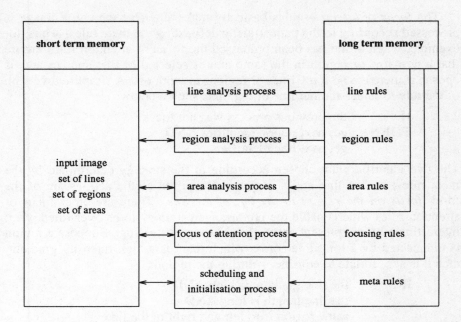

Figure 10.1 Rule based segmentation

corresponding processes: see below for more detail.

The *meta rules* ensure that the initialisation process is carried out at the start of processing. For example:

IF	regions are absent
THEN	initialise regions

IF	lines are absent
THEN	initialise lines

IF	areas are absent
THEN	generate areas

They also perform more subtle tasks to create an appropriate control strategy. For example, if there is an area with low average uniformity of regions, then the priority of the region analyser rules will be adjusted so that those which split regions are given a higher priority than those which merge regions. The original thesis (Nazif 1983) should be consulted for fuller details of the various strategies. Meta rules also stop the analysis when segmentation is complete.

The *focus of attention* rules basically make sure that the entire image is processed according to the path strategy defined by the meta rules. Thus, for example, when a line has been processed the focus of attention rules ensure that a new line or region in the same area is selected or that another area is chosen if there are no more lines or regions to work on. A simplified version of the rule to select another line or region is shown below:

> **IF**   the previous process was not focus
> **THEN**   get next region identifier **AND**
>   get next line identifier

The two identifiers are chosen according to the strategy determined by the meta rules; both a line and a region are required as the actions are of the form *focus on the region to the left of the line*. There are other focus of attention rules which enable the pre-arranged strategy to be over-ruled when interesting patterns present themselves during processing. Suppose a region is intersected by a long line across which there is a high intensity gradient, then it is appropriate to consider splitting the region:

> **IF**   the line gradient is high **AND**
>   the line length is long **AND**
>   same region is to left and right of the line
> **THEN**   focus on the region to the left of the line

We now turn to the processes which are active one at a time. A newly activated process looks at its corresponding rule set and selects the one with highest priority which is also enabled. To do this it has to look up values in short term memory. The action side of the rule consists of some function in the invoking process which usually updates the short term memory. Once the action is finished the process tries to match the rule with next highest priority and so on. When no more rules match in a given process, control passes to the next level of rule set; for example when the region analyser has executed all matching rules, a focus rule may be activated to select another region, line or area for attention. Alternatively, if all the appropriate focus of attention rules have been matched, then a meta rule will decide which process to bring in next or to terminate the entire analysis. Overall the control is *data driven* or forward chaining: the characteristics of the original image determined the initial creation of regions, lines and areas, plus the allocation of priority to rules by the meta-rules.

Region Analysis Rules

The purpose of the region analysis process is to see whether the current region under investigation can be improved by splitting or merging. If there are two regions with the same intensity, or in the case of a colour image the same intensities for all three colours, then they should be merged. The following rule accomplishes this:

> **IF**   the red levels show low difference between the
> two regions **AND**
> similarly for blue **AND**
> similarly for green
> **THEN** merge the two regions

In order to deal with noise in the image, we are looking for a very small region surrounded by another of similar colour and intensity:

> **IF**   the region size is very low **AND**
> the adjacency with another region is high **AND**
> the red levels show low difference between the
> two regions **AND**
> similarly for blue **AND**
> similarly for green
> **THEN** merge the two regions

Another possibility is that sometimes regions will be created at the boundary between two other regions whose average intensities are markedly different. These "hybrid" regions can be created as a result of the mathematical averaging process rather than because of some feature in the scene; pixels near the boundary simply do not get categorised as belonging to one or other of the main regions. They are characterised by small size, high gradient (of intensity), and a high aspect ratio. Although other cases exist, the rule below indicates how these hybrids are detected and merged out.

> **IF**   the region size is low **AND**
> the region average gradient is high **AND**
> the red levels do not show high difference
> between the two regions **AND**
> similarly for blue **AND**
> similarly for green
> **THEN** merge the two regions

Sometimes when several regions intersect at the same place low image resolution results in the creation of a spurious region. The following removes them:

> **IF**   the region size is low **AND**
> the number of adjacent regions is high **AND**
> the adjacent region size is not low **AND**

the red levels do not show high difference
between the two regions **AND**
similarly for blue **AND**
similarly for green
THEN   merge the two regions

Nazif's system deals with splitting regions through histogram analysis (discussed in Chapter 5) and through consideration of lines which pass through a single region. Two corresponding rules are:

IF   the region histogram is bimodal
THEN   split the region according to the histogram

IF   the region size is low **AND**
the line bisects the region **AND**
the line length is not low **AND**
the line average gradient is high
THEN   split the region at lines

Line Analysis Rules

There are rather more actions that can be taken on lines than regions. We examine continuity, closure and proximity of lines and regions in order to join, extend, merge or delete lines.

There are many cases for joining lines, the simplest being when there is a line with an open end and another line a short distance away in front.

IF   the line end point is open **AND**
the distance to the line in front is low
THEN   join the lines by forward expansion

A similar case allows for backward expansion. There are several cases when adjacent regions provide clues for joining lines. The simplest case is shown in Figure 10.2. The corresponding rule is:

IF   the line end point is open **AND**
the line gradient is not very low **AND**
the distance to the line in front is not very high **AND**
the two lines have the same region to the left **AND**
the two lines have the same region to the right
THEN   join the lines by forward expansion

Sometimes a line will not have any close neighbours, but if it has reasonable average gradient and is not too short, then it is quite likely to correspond to a scene feature. The tactics are to extend it and hope that eventually some other rule fires which will provide a suitable cause of

Figure 10.2 Two lines to be joined

action. The rule to extend such a line is:

> **IF**   the line end point is open **AND**
>   the line average gradient is not low **AND**
>   the line length is not low
> **THEN**   extend the line forward

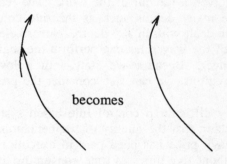

becomes

Figure 10.3 Two lines to merge

When a line is extended it may eventually reach another one as shown in Figure 10.3. This case could also arise from the initial creation of lines. To merge the two lines, we could use the following rule:

> **IF**   the line length is not low **AND**
>   the length of the line in front is low **AND**
>   the lines are touching **AND**
>   the closest point in front is very low distance away
> **THEN**   merge the lines forward

Finally we mention an example of line deletion. A very short line with weak gradient may well be due to noise factors and could be deleted thus:

> **IF**   the line length is very low **AND**
>   the line average gradient is low

THEN   delete the line

Area Control

Areas are created during initialisation, but are then monitored during further processing. Texture, see Chapter 8, provides an important clue, and rules are available to create and add to areas considered to be *smooth* or *textured*. Another criterion used is to look for lines which encircle an area or almost do so. During processing an area may have its texture changed to and from smooth, or an area may be *frozen* to stop further work, and some areas may be deleted altogether.

Discussion

This overview has given a flavour of the work. The reader should bear in mind that there are many details such as the rule conditions themselves which have not been dealt with in any depth. Nevertheless, there should be some appreciation of the way rules can perform the segmentation in a forward chaining manner. Because we start with a low-level image and proceed to extract regions, we can also consider the processing here to be *bottom-up*.

It is always very difficult to control rule based systems, and although Nazif and Levine claim that the quality of segmentation is good, they acknowledge that a heavy price has been paid in execution time. Rule based segmentation was about five times as time consuming as a split and merge algorithm, and about twice as expensive as histogram segmentation.

There is other work on rules for operating on regions and lines (Adorni et al., 1985, Adorni et al., 1987).

We now examine another system which analyses natural colour scenes. However because there is a high level model, albeit very crude, of what the scene looks like, it can adopt more scene specific processing strategies.

A Bottom-up and Top-down Region Analyser

This system was actually developed before Nazif and Levine undertook their study (Ohta et al., 1979.). The points we highlight (Ohta 1985) here are concerned with the use of semantic information in the segmentation and use of bottom-up and top-down processing. Bottom-up methods create areas for focusing attention during top-down model-driven analysis.

The objective of the system is to take a raw image and return an analysis of it in terms of a scene description illustrated in Figure 10.4. At the top level there is a description of the *scene* including details of the horizon; this

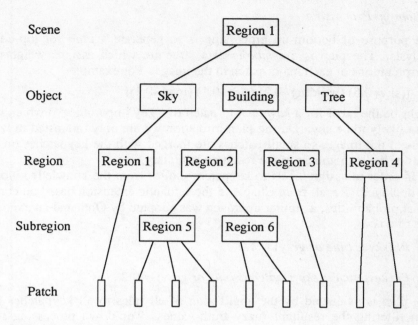

Figure 10.4 The Scene Description

is then broken down into the *objects* identified in the scene, for example sky or buildings. Each object is then decomposed into *regions* which represent the main parts such as the walls of the building. *Sub-regions* refer to smaller parts of objects such as windows; this division is somewhat subjective but it affects processing because worrying about a window, for example, will not affect the boundary between the sky and building whereas the converse may not be true. *Patches* are groups of pixels having coherent pictorial properties, but which have not yet got a semantic interpretation.

The model of the scene about which the system can reason is held in a special purpose semantic network. It is more restricted than the nets considered in Chapter 9 because it holds all the rules in a manner which permit fast processing: this idea of partitioning the rule-set was first encountered in Nazif and Levine's system. The network nodes are called *knowledge blocks* and contain rules about the entity they represent. There are approximately 60 rules in the whole system, but their structure varies depending upon their role.

Bottom-up Processing

The purpose of bottom-up processing is to generate a *plan* for top-down analysis. The plan is a *symbolic* data structure which assigns weights to interpretations of each major patch in the image. For example

[(sky=0.5) (building=0.2) (tree=0.1) (road=0.1)]

might be the label for a *keypatch* (a patch of "key importance") which was most likely to be sky. During plan formation we are only interested in large areas of the image, so small patches are merged with the keypatches on the basis of the smoothness of the resultant boundary.

In order to assign labels to keypatches, rules from the knowledge blocks are deployed. Recall from Chapter 5 the semantic extension based on conditional probabilities; a similar approach was adopted by Ohta and an example of a rule is:

Pr (sky is blue or grey) = 1.0

Pr (keypatch is sky | patch is blue or grey) = 0.2

The plan is evaluated by the application of all rules to all keypatches and then filtering the resultant fuzzy truth-values. Top-down processing then takes over.

Top-down Analysis

The objective of the top-down phase is to assign a definite interpretation to each patch. Not only are the rules effectively separated into sets, or knowledge blocks, depending upon their semantic net position, they are also divided into *global* and *local* sets. The global rules assign interpretations to keypatches; the others deal with lower-level entities, windows for example, which will have no effect on the overall arrangement of the keypatches. Whenever certain key global events are executed, such as to determine the horizon, the current top-down model and working data is discarded and a new plan is generated by the bottom-up process. Control then returns to the top-down part.

The action part of rules are mainly to perform one or more of the following operations: assign a label to a patch; create or merge a region using a patch; create or merge an object using a region; and link a new object into the scene. Normally attached to these actions is a confidence factor, and in fact when a rule fires it puts its action onto an *agenda* for actual subsequent execution. The highest-confidence agenda-item belonging to an appropriate knowledge block is selected and executed. (If there are no items at all, processing terminates). If the action is to interpret a keypatch, then all the global rules for the remaining un-interpreted keypatches are activated (or re-activated). If the action is to interpret a patch, then the local rules for the current patch and those corresponding to touching patches are activated (or re-activated); recall the algorithm described in Chapter 5 (Feldman & Yakimovsky, 1974) which also updated its "confidences" as a result of neighbouring regions being "interpreted".

The overall top-down process is thus focussed to work on the interpretation of keypatches and within that on local interpretations. Patches and keypatches have their interpretation "fixed" if there is sufficient relative confidence in them. Whenever a patch interpretation is actually executed, all agenda items giving an inconsistent interpretation to the patch are deleted. A patch is never re-examined once labelled, ("wrong" labels are erased on plan re-evaluation). Sometimes these fixing events will cause a complete regeneration of the plan. Figure 10.5 shows the flow of control between the top-down and bottom-up processes.

Discussion

We have seen here the use of rules which are model based. In this case the model is *image* based, but this does not matter as there are no spatial relations to be processed bar those of the type "the sky is above the building". The bottom-up part of the system is clearly forward chaining, although there is a slight hint of backward chaining in the top-down process. In backward chaining we reason that to interpret the scene we interpret each object, that to interpret an object we interpret its regions, and so on. However, the order in which this is done is such that several competing interpretations are conducted in parallel until a good "fix" is found. Good here means "nothing better at this time". A more recent system built for similar scenes employs a blackboard so as to achieve goal-directed with some data-driven control (Kohl et al., 1987).

Generic Model-based Vision

We now turn our attention to the inferencing procedure adopted for the ACRONYM system which is of interest for several reasons. It gives examples of the use of important Artificial Intelligence techniques such as constraint propagation, backward chaining production systems, and the generation of predictive hypotheses. It is also an example of the application of generalised cones (Binford 1971) mentioned in Chapters 8 and 9. The objective of the system is to interpret images containing generic objects, such as wide-bodied aircraft, in a way which can be generalised to work for many classes of object.

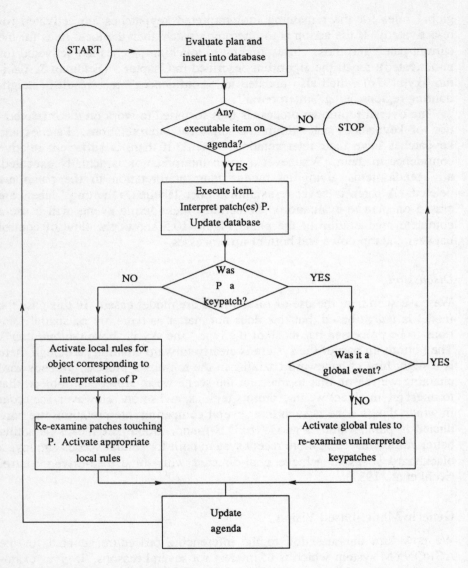

Figure 10.5 The flow of Ohta's program

In outline the system uses its database of objects to generate observability graphs which contain predictions of what to look for in order to find each object. The matcher performs an interpretation of the observability graph from a processed form of the image (Brooks et al., 1979).

Geometric Reasoning

A central feature of ACRONYM is the way it reasons about the position of objects in space. Recall from the discussion in the previous Chapter that each object can be stored in the sub-parts hierarchy as a set of frame units together with the associated affixment tree to represent the spatial relationships. Every object has its own local co-ordinate system, and mappings between one local system and another are made by transformations. In other words the objects are *constrained* to fit together. More generally if we have a collection of un-constrained objects, say a camera and a cube, we can apply constraints to indicate for example that the cube is in the field of view of the camera. We can solve the set of constraints to find a subset of space in which all the constraints hold, ie the cube is in view; this subset is called the *satisfying set*. In some trivial cases finding this set can be performed by the Simplex linear programming method. For example, when reasoning about the locations of rectangular planar objects on a planar surface, the constraints are all linear; this is left as an exercise for the reader.

A constraint manipulation system (Brooks 1981) performs the demanding task of reasoning about constraints to produce the satisfying set. If the set is empty, then the constraints are inconsistent, i.e. we have a contradiction. However because the proof procedure is not complete, we can only say that something does not hold, not the converse. As an example of how this can be used, consider occlusions of objects within the visible volume of a camera (Brooks 1983). The volume can be represented as an infinite pyramid with circular cross section extending from the focal point of the camera, see Figure 10.6. In order to say that the objects definitely lie within the volume, constraints are added to them. Now to test for occlusions, pairs of objects are selected: constraints are added to assert that one object never occludes the other. If the satisfying set becomes empty, then by contradiction we know that the object was definitely at least partially occluded. If we cannot get an empty set, then we know by the partial proof procedure that the object *may* be visible.

Prediction

The prediction process is driven by an essentially backward chaining production system of about 280 rules (Brooks 1983). What it does is work breadth-first along and down the sub-parts hierarchy. It thus starts with the most general description of a part, and generates an observation graph for it. This contains cues for the matcher based on those features of the part which are invariant with position. For example, if a feature is collinear in the

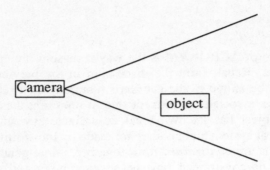

Figure 10.6 An object in view of a camera

model, it will also be so in the image. Therefore it should be added to the graph. Parallel features in the model also produce parallel lines in the image provided they are observable. Connectivity is another invariant which is used in the observation graphs. The nodes of the graph are actually *ribbons*: i.e. a planar shape described by a straight-line spine, a line segment cross-section and a sweeping rule. Ribbons have useful properties which facilitate mappings between image features and generalised cones. The arcs of the graph correspond to relations between ribbons.

Having made predictions for objects at one level in the sub-parts hierarchy, interpretation takes place using the matcher. Then the next level is brought in to refine the predictions, and so on. Thus more and more constraints are brought in as processing proceeds, and gradually a tree is constructed to represent the different lines of interpretation.

Discussion

ACRONYM is a complex piece of software consisting of many difficult modules. The coverage here has been limited to a few major issues. The *world* based object models are interesting, but really need the geometric reasoning to support them. They may not be so effective for natural scenes, but work well in the more artificial environments that industrial robot Vision is likely to be used. The work on geometric reasoning is hard, and is an area worthy of a book in its own right.

What we have seen here is an example of a backward chaining system, that uses hierarchical matching. One side effect of this approach is that ACRONYM can tell the implications of particular inferences. For an example consider an application to detect wide-bodied aircraft from an aerial photograph of an airport, where the height of the camera was unknown. The conclusion was that if the camera height was within one range then there were wide-bodied aircraft at two locations, whereas if the camera was in another height range (decided by the system of course) then another aircraft was a wide-bodied vehicle (otherwise it was too big).

We have also seen the generation of observable features of objects for subsequent testing by the matcher. For a compiled approach to prediction see Burns and Kitchen (Burns & Kitchen, 1987). Finally, we have seen an example of the practical application of a theorem prover which is not complete. When asked if a satisfying set for a set of constraints is empty, the constraint manipulation system returns outcomes corresponding to *empty* or *I don't know*.

Conclusion

In this Chapter we first examined the concept of a production system and then examined some practical examples. One system reasoned exclusively about regions (Ohta), another only about lines (Brooks) and the third took account of both boundaries and regions (Nazif and Levine). On the whole the lower level tasks are performed by forward chaining methods, whereas backward chaining approaches have been found to be useful when high level models of the expected scene exist.

Rule based systems can be seen to be powerful in terms of flexibility and quality of output. However there is often a high price to be paid in terms of processing costs. For efficiency reasons the rule set is often partitioned into semantically related subsets.

Another major distinction between systems is the basis of the model: image or world based. The latter provide greater flexibility but at a cost of performing expensive and difficult geometric reasoning. All the models we have seen have been hand generated, but in the future automatic conversion from CAD system output will be common. Hence there will be a link into automatic parts handling and inspection. The future, commercially, lies in these applications.

Perhaps the biggest challenge is for systems to be able to make intelligent deductions and observations about situations they have never seen before. The field is ripe for original research in this area!

Exercises

(1) Recall Figure 10.6; label the relevant lines in it as in Figure 10.7. Formulate the planar arrangement of camera and object in this Figure as a linear program. Explore its use to determine whether the object is in view of the camera.

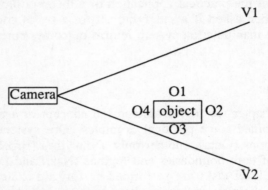

Figure 10.7 An object in view of a camera

(2) Use the frames created in Exercise 9.1 parts (i) and (ii) to predict ribbons to match with the dinner table shown in Figure 4.13. Attempt a match by hand. (Be very generous in what you allow the "ribbons" to be.)

(3) Investigate how we might perceive the "invisible" table edge in Figures 1.1 and 4.13 using the definition for the table top created in Exercise 9.1 part (iii).

CHAPTER 11

Epilogue

The Preface to this book introduced it as an attempt to give an elementary account of what Computer Vision involves; to provide the vocabulary and a grounding on which advanced study could be built. It used some definitions and concepts whose meaning may only be clear now that the reader has digested the intervening ten Chapters. It is worth therefore reiterating that this book is, after all, only a "First Course", and its omissions are probably every bit as notable as the material that has been covered; we hope, though, that you are now well placed to fill in the gaps in your knowledge. Here we will run through the main topics that we think have been left out in trying to keep the book short, but which should be explored by any serious student of the discipline.

Edge detection was explained only briefly, and the ideas presented are, by today's standards, very simple. In the 1970's, Marr and Hildreth (Marr & Hildreth, 1980) advanced this part of the science beyond the "first order" approach of Sobel etc. It has been remarked that many modern Vision systems base their low level work on the *Canny* edge detector (Canny 1986). Canny attempted a computational approach to edge detection - his work is a major achievement that won him a Ph.D., and we did not attempt to summarise it. Canny's is not the only modern detector - there is still active work in deriving new edge and corner detectors (Noble 1987).

Our study of segmentation was merely a selection from a wide field. Certainly the Hough transform is essential knowledge for anyone working in this area, but a complete survey of other segmentation techniques would occupy more than one book. As is so often the case, the correct solution to the problem in hand is usually application dependent; while simple thresholding works for some, region growers are necessary for others, and yet other techniques are necessary in yet other applications. Precisely what the segmentation is trying to achieve is all important; optical character recognition systems want to identify characters (uniquely), while an automatic traffic census system would need only to count moving vehicles. It is not surprising that their requirements will be different.

We barely scratched the surface of 3D feature extraction. While stereo is a proven and popular idea, the extraction of 3D information from motion is also widely used. The student is advised to follow any of the quoted references, particularly Ullman (Ullman 1979) for a deeper introduction. The other "Shape from ..." techniques are also worthy of further study - each is a large area in itself.

We stated early on that many of the algorithms in this book lend themselves to exploitation by parallel hardware. With the advent of more accessible and efficient parallel machines, in particular transputers, this is ever more the case (Dew 1988). Much of the load of, eg, edge detectors can be dismissed if the algorithm does not have to be executed "serially". Current technology can, for example, execute the very costly Canny edge detector in "real time" (Ruff 1987) (that is, as fast as the refresh rate of the image acquisition equipment).

We have mentioned David Marr and his pioneering work more than once. Marr constructed a computational theory of the Vision process. He developed a vocabulary of the subject, Primal Sketch (loosely, the output of the low level processes), 2.5D sketch (the result of segmentation - halfway between a 2D and 3D description) etc., that is frequently used in Vision literature. Any serious student of Computer Vision should make a study of Marr's work an early priority.

Our study of WISARD in many ways begs more questions than it answers. In a very short time in the future we would no doubt have described a Parallel Distributed Processing (PDP) machine. The very rapidly advancing field of Connectionist Machines (McClelland & Rumelhart 1986) could easily extend to cover a book (we have cited some), but this would not be appropriate for this level of text. We can be sure that, in future, however much Connectionist and conventional Vision approaches diverge there will be a move towards more adaptive systems which will be able to learn things from their environment and past mistakes. We might also have included something on the progress being made in the understanding of natural vision systems (Changeux 1987), as they will almost certainly contain clues for building better artificial Vision mechanisms.

With the falling cost of hardware, much more attention is being paid to the processing of colour images. The examples we have given of systems that happen to use colour do not really indicate the advantages and disadvantages of this additional information; certainly, as colour imaging equipment becomes more widespread, so will be the requirement for algorithms that exploit it. A good example of current work in colour is a colour edge finder (Forsyth 1987). We have also paid no attention to the field of pictorial databases (Bolc 1984). As storage and display devices drop in price, so these systems will become common. They will have potentially demanding requirements for knowledge representation, which will be helped by the provision of powerful Vision oriented tools. Much more could have been said about the various representation ideas (B-reps, CSG etc.); we can only hope we have given a flavour of how a powerful method, in the case we examined generalised cones, can be used in limited domains.

Finally, many Vision systems work in the context of robotics. We have not studied many specific Vision applications, but automatic inspection and passive navigation of a robot are (relatively) well known. Topics such as these are worthy of study, but they will build on the fundamental ideas that we hope have been adequately covered here.

APPENDIX I

Some C functions

For the sake of example, here are two C functions that implement some of the simpler algorithms that have been presented. The C language (Kernighan & Ritchie, 1978) is very well suited to the lower level programming required for Image Processing; there is a lot of array addressing and the optimum performance is wanted, for which the low level nature of C is ideal.

These routines should compile and run under most C compilers. The library and system calls presumed available are *free* and *malloc*. These will almost certainly be found on Unix* systems or Unix lookalike systems.

For the sake of simplicity there is no input or output shown here; we assume that the "image" to be processed is held in memory in the array *data*, and that the integer variables *width*, *length* and *depth* contain its horizontal and vertical dimensions and number of grey levels respectively. The pixels are presumed to be presented in row by row order. Another assumption is that the number of intensity levels is less than or equal to 256, so that each pixel may be represented by 1 byte; *data* is of type *unsigned char* (which is usually an 8 bit quantity) accordingly.

The aim of these codes is to demonstrate how some simple algorithms may be implemented, and there is no suggestion that the functions are in any way optimal. Where corners have not been cut for speed, it is for the sake of clarity.

Histogram Equalisation

Function *eq* takes the input data array with its dimensions and calculates the best grey level transformation it can to equalise the intensity histogram (see Chapter 4). The pointer to the image resulting from applying the transformation is returned.

---

*Unix is a trademark of Bell Laboratories.

152

```
unsigned char *
eq(data,height,width,depth)
unsigned char *data;
int height,width,depth;
/*
 * eq equalises histograms.  The input parameters are
 *
 *        data      an unsigned char array of pixels
 *        height    the vertical image dimension
 *        width     the horizontal image dimension
 *        depth     the number of grey levels (< = 256)
 *
 * The function returns a pointer to the equalised array
 */
{
        /*
         * Local variables:
         *
         *        N         integer to hold byte size of image
         *        cp        scratch unsigned char pointer
         *        freq      integer array to compile histogram
         *        i         scratch integer
         *        t         integer array to hold mapping
         *        tdata     unsigned char array to hold output
         *        factor    float to hold depth/N
         *
         */
        /*
         * malloc reserves the array space we need; the one
         * argument is the number of bytes required, so array
         * size is multiplied by datatype size.
         * We assume (possibly incorrectly) that the space so
         * returned is erased to zeroes
         */
        unsigned char
                *cp,*tdata;
        int     *freq = (int *) malloc((unsigned) depth * sizeof(int)),
                *t = (int *) malloc((unsigned) depth * sizeof(int)),
                N = width*height,i;
        float   factor = (float) depth / (float) N;
        /*
         * Compile the histogram of the input image
```

```
*/
cp = data;
i = N;
while (i--)
        (freq[(int) *cp++])++;
/*
 * Determine the mapping as the cumulative histogram is
 * calculated.  Floating point numbers must be rounded
 * not truncated, so we do
 *        [integer] = (int) ([floating point] + 0.5);
 * and assume the coercion truncates.
 */
if (freq[0])
        t[0] = (int) ((float) freq[0] * factor + 0.5) - 1;
else
        t[0] = 0;
for (i=1; i<depth; i++) {
        /*
         * form cumulative frequency
         */
        freq[i] += freq[i-1];
        if (freq[i])
                t[i] = (int) ((float) freq[i] * factor + 0.5) - 1;
        else
                t[i] = 0;
}
/*
 * Assign the space for the output image, and perform the
 * mapping
 */
tdata = (unsigned char *)
        malloc((unsigned) N * sizeof(unsigned char));
cp = tdata;
while (N--)
        *cp++ = (unsigned char) t[*data++];
/*
 * Release space no longer required
 */
free((char *) freq);
free((char *) t);
return(tdata);

}
```

Figure 4.6 shows an example use of this algorithm.

Hierarchical Edge Detection

Function *py* takes the input data array with its dimensions and a proposed "level" of pyramid (see Chapter 5). It checks that there are the requisite number of factors of 2 in the image dimensions to permit the coarser images to be formed without data truncation (this would be a trivial feature to amend if deemed necessary) and forms the image pyramid. The recursive function *refine* is applied at each pixel of the top layer so formed; this calls a boundary test *bndry* and the function recurses down the pyramid if the boundary strength exceeds some threshold *thresh - thresh* will be dependent on the underlying edge operator, image contrast and any number of possible image features.

The actual edge operator is encapsulated in routine *edge*, with a general purpose calling interface, allowing simple amendment of the operator - the code that follows implements a Sobel edge operator.

The performance of the algorithm for different depths of pyramid can be tested by including in the program a global counter that is incremented on each call to *bndry*. The routine returns a pointer to an array of the same dimensions as *data* that contains the edge strength in pixels thought to correspond to edges, and zeroes elsewhere. Two external variables communicate with the calling program; *thresh* has been described, and *max* (presumed initialised to zero) contains the maximum edge strength seen, and hence the maximum intensity level in the output image.

```
/*
 * 3 functions support the action of py;
 *
 *      py        is the called function
 *      refine    recurses over likely pixels
 *      bndry     is a (boolean) boundary test
 *      edge      is an edge operator
 *
 */
/*
 * The macro AVERAGE provides as an unsigned char the mean
 * of four arguments.
 *
 * NULL is used as a null pointer.
 */
#define AVERAGE(a,b,c,d) (unsigned char) (((int)(a)+(int)(b)+(int)(c)+(int)(d))/4)
```

```
#define   NULL   0

/*
 * Variables global to the file;
 *
 *         max      an externally defined integer, initialised to 0
 *         thresh   an externally defined integer
 *         pyramid  to point at an array of images
 *         out      to hold the output image
 *
 */
extern int
          max,thresh;
static unsigned char
          **pyramid,*out;

unsigned char *
py(data,height,width,level)
unsigned char *data;
int height,width,level;
/*
 * py is a hierarchical edge detector. The input parameters are
 *
 *         data     an unsigned char array of pixels
 *         height   the vertical image dimension
 *         width    the horizontal image dimension
 *         level    the number of pyramid layers to generate (>=1)
 *
 * The function returns a pointer to an edge array
 */
{
          /*
           * Local variables:
           *
           *         N        integer to hold byte size of image
           *         cp1      scratch unsigned char pointer
           *         cp2      scratch unsigned char pointer
           *         cp3      scratch unsigned char pointer
           *         i,j,k,x  scratch integers
           *
           */
          /*
```

```
 * malloc reserves the array space we need; the one
 * argument is the number of bytes required, so array
 * size is multiplied by datatype size.
 * We assume (possibly incorrectly) that the space so
 * returned is erased to zeroes
 */
int        N = width*height,i,j,k,x;
unsigned char
           *cp1,*cp2,*cp3;
/*
 * Check level parameter is sensible.
 * Check 2's divisibility of dimensions.
 * NULL return indicates failure.
 */
if (level<1)
           return(NULL);
if ((height!=(height>>level)<<level) ||
   (width!=(width>>level)<<level))
           return(NULL);
/*
 * Ensure top level has sides >= 3
 */
while (height>>level <= 2)
           level--;
while (width>>level <= 2)
           level--;
/*
 * Make space for the pointers and the output.
 */
pyramid = (unsigned char **)
           malloc((unsigned) level * sizeof(unsigned char *));
out = (unsigned char *)
           malloc((unsigned) N * sizeof(unsigned char));
/*
 * Bottom layer is the input image.
 */
pyramid[0] = data;
for (i=1; i<level; i++) {
           /*
            * Build the layers. At each layer, divide
            * dimensions by two, and area by four.
            */
```

```
            x = width;
            width >>= 1;
            height >>= 1;
            N >>= 2;
            *(pyramid+i) = (unsigned char *)
                    malloc((unsigned) N * sizeof(unsigned char));
            /*
            * cp1 points to one row, cp2 the next.  cp3
            * points to pixels in next layer up.
            */
            /*
            * This code is not at all optimal; it is
            * written to be understood!
            */
            cp1 = *(pyramid+i-1);
            cp2 = cp1+x;
            cp3 = *(pyramid+i);
            for (j=0; j<height; j++) {
                    for (k=0; k<width; k++) {
                            *cp3++ =
                                AVERAGE(*cp1,*(cp1+1),*cp2, *(cp2+1));
                            cp1 += 2;
                            cp2 += 2;
                    }
                    cp1 += x;
                    cp2 += x;
            }
    }
    /*
    * Now the layers exist.  Initiate "refine"
    * at each pixel of the top layer.
    */
    for (i=0; i<height; i++)
            for (j=0; j<width; j++)
                    /*
                    * Remember the layers are numbered
                    * 0,1, ... ,(level-1)
                    */
                    refine(level-1,j,i,height,width);
    /*
    * Give back space no longer needed.
    */
```

```
        for (i=1; i<level; i++)
                    free((char *) *(pyramid+i));
        free((char *) pyramid);
        return(out);
}


static
refine(level,x,y,height,width)
int level,x,y,height,width;
/*
 * refine recurses at strong edge evidence.
 * The input parameters are
 *
 *          height    the vertical image dimension
 *          level     the level of the pyramid at which we are
 *          width     the horizontal image dimension
 *          x,y       image coordinates
 *
 * At the bottom image, we set an output pixel.  At
 * higher images, we recurse down if the function "bndry"
 * returns TRUE.
 */
{
        int i = bndry(level,x,y,height,width);
        if (i) {
                if (level==0) {
                        /*
                         * Set a pixel, and remember maximum.
                         */
                        *(out+y*width+x) = (unsigned char) i;
                        if (i>max)
                                    max = i;
                        return;
                }
                /*
                 * Look at the four pixels below.
                 */
                refine(level-1,2*x,2*y,2*height,2*width);
                refine(level-1,2*x+1,2*y,2*height,2*width);
                refine(level-1,2*x,2*y+1,2*height,2*width);
                refine(level-1,2*x+1,2*y+1,2*height,2*width);
        }
```

```
}

static
bndry(level,x,y,height,width)
int level,x,y,height,width;
/*
 * bndry returns TRUE if the pixel it is asked
 * to look at has a high ''edge'' strength.  The input
 * parameters are
 *
 *        height    the vertical image dimension
 *        level     the level of the pyramid at which we are
 *        width     the horizontal image dimension
 *        x,y       image coordinates
 *
 */
{
         int i = edge(*(pyramid+level),x,y,height,width);
         if (i > thresh)
                  return(i);
         else
                  return(0);
}

static
edge(data,x,y,height,width)
unsigned char *data;
int x,y,height,width;
/*
 * edge is an edge operator.  The input parameters are
 *
 *        data      an unsigned char pixel array
 *        height    the vertical image dimension
 *        width     the horizontal image dimension
 *        x,y       image coordinates
 *
 * The interface to ''edge'' is general purpose enough to
 * allow any simple edge operator to be put here.  The
 * code that follows implements a Sobel operator,
 * and returns the edge strength as the sum of
 * the magnitudes of the X and Y direction strengths, normalised
 * to lie in the range of the image grey levels.
```

```
*/
{
        /*
         * Local variables:
         *
         *      str        integer to accumulate strength
         *      tmp        scratch integer
         *      cp1,cp2    scratch unsigned char pointers
         */
        int         str,tmp;
        unsigned char
                    *cp1,*cp2;
        /*
         * Return no evidence at image perimeter
         */
        if (x==0 || y==0 || x==(width-1) || (y==height-1))
                return(0);
        /*
         * cp1 points just North West of target pixel
         * cp2 points just South West of target pixel
         */
        cp1 = data+(y-1)*width+(x-1);
        cp2 = data+(y+1)*width+(x-1);
        /*
         * Calculate vertical edge strength;  Store
         * magnitude.
         */
        tmp = (*cp2 + *(cp2+1)*2 + (*cp2+2)) -
                (*cp1 + *(cp1+1)*2 + (*cp1+2));
        str = (tmp<0 ? -tmp : tmp);
        /*
         * cp1 still points just North West of target pixel
         * cp2 points just North East of target pixel
         */
        cp2 = cp1+2;
        /*
         * Calculate horizontal edge strength;  Add to
         * magnitude.
         */
        tmp = (*cp2 + *(cp2+width)*2 + (*cp2+2*width)) -
                (*cp1 + *(cp1+width)*2 + (*cp1+2*width));
        if (tmp<0)
```

```
            str -= tmp;
      else
            str += tmp;
      /*
      * Maximum strength is 8*maximum grey level
      */
      return(str/8);
}
```

Figures 5.7 and 7.2 show some examples of the use of this algorithm.

APPENDIX II

Fourier Theory

The study of Fourier transforms is well established, and many excellent and thorough references exist (Gonzalez & Wintz, 1987). As remarked in Chapter 4, Fourier theory is an important part of Image Processing; this book has not the space to give a full presentation, and it is not appropriate anyway. Here will be presented the definitions and basic results associated with the transform; Chapter 4 contained an overview of why these results are important in the processing of images.

Definitions

The Fourier transform of a function of one variable $f(x)$ is given by

$$F(u) = \int_{-\infty}^{\infty} f(x)\exp(-i\,2\pi ux)dx$$

which generalises in two dimensions to

$$F(u,v) = \int_{-\infty}^{\infty}\int_{-\infty}^{\infty} f(x,y)\exp[-i\,2\pi(ux+vy)]dxdy$$

It is seen immediately that the transform of a function is a *complex* function, while the function itself may be real.

The inverse transform is similar;

$$f(x) = \int_{-\infty}^{\infty} F(u)\exp(i\,2\pi ux)du$$

and

$$f(x,y) = \int_{-\infty}^{\infty}\int_{-\infty}^{\infty} F(u,v)\exp[i\,2\pi(ux+vy)]dudv$$

The variables u and v are often referred to as the *frequency variables*.

Writing

$$F(u,v) = R(u,v) + iI(u,v)$$

where R and I are *real* valued functions, associated definitions are the

163

Fourier Spectrum

$$|F(u,v)| = [R^2(u,v) + I^2(u,v)]^{\frac{1}{2}}$$

and *Fourier Phase*

$$\Phi(u,v) = \tan^{-1}\left[\frac{I(u,v)}{R(u,v)}\right]$$

Being real valued, it is possible to plot the Fourier spectrum of a 2 dimensional transform - see Figure II.1 for an example. Notice its rotational symmetry about the origin, a feature of the spectrum of the transform. The bright spots at the centre represent low frequencies, and the bright points remote from the centre represent the higher frequencies.

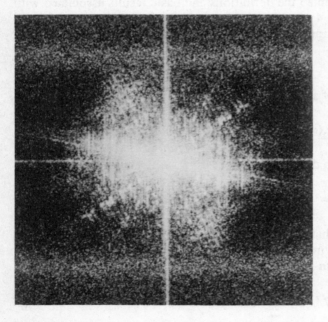

Figure II.1 The Fourier power spectrum of Figure 4.16

Companion definitions exist for *discrete* functions; if we suppose values of f are given at $f(x_0+x\,\delta x, y_0+y\,\delta y)$ for $x=0,1,...,M-1$ and $y=0,1,...,N-1$ and we write

$$f(x,y) = f(x_0+x\,\delta x, y_0+y\,\delta y)$$

for convenience, then the discrete transform and its inverse are given by

$$F(u,v) = \frac{1}{MN} \sum_{x=0}^{M-1} \sum_{y=0}^{N-1} f(x,y) \exp\left[-i\,2\pi(\frac{ux}{M}+\frac{vy}{N})\right] \qquad \text{II.1}$$

$$f(x,y) = \sum_{u=0}^{M-1} \sum_{v=0}^{N-1} F(u,v) \exp\left[i\,2\pi(\frac{ux}{M}+\frac{vy}{N})\right]$$

We have now side stepped all problems associated with the integration by dealing with numerical computation only; it should be clear that digital images fit into these formulae very easily.

Properties

Given two functions $f(x,y)$ and $g(x,y)$, their *convolution*, written $f*g$ is given by

$$f(x,y)*g(x,y) = \int_{-\infty}^{\infty}\int_{-\infty}^{\infty} f(\alpha,\beta)g(x-\alpha,y-\beta)d\alpha d\beta$$

and their *correlation*, written fog is given by

$$f(x,y)og(x,y) = \int_{-\infty}^{\infty}\int_{-\infty}^{\infty} f(\alpha,\beta)g(x+\alpha,y+\beta)d\alpha d\beta$$

(Discrete definitions follow similarly). Both of these are very costly to compute yet both are very commonly required in Image Processing. Correlation we have seen in Chapter 4, and convolution appears implicitly in a range of edge enhancement and frequency manipulation filters. It is a result beyond the scope of this book to show that both can be performed (relatively) cheaply in the Fourier domain; writing $T(f)$ for the Fourier transform of f, the *convolution theorem* states that if

$$F = T(f) \qquad \text{and} \qquad G = T(g)$$

then

$$T(f*g) = F.G$$

and

$$f.g = T^{-1}(F*G)$$

while the *correlation theorem* states that

$$T(fog) = F.G^{*}$$

and

$$f \cdot g^* = \mathbf{T}^{-1}(FoG)$$

(where g^* denotes the complex conjugate of g).

Why these results are true is not important here, but their implications should be understood since the two theorems permit very expensive filtering operations to be performed in the Fourier domain at lower cost, since they reduce both convolution and correlation to simple function products; that is, to perform a convolution of an image represented by (digital) function $f(x,y)$, we can transform the function to $F(u,v)$, multiply by some appropriate function $G(u,v)$ and determine the inverse transform of FG, which will represent the convolution of f with the function whose transform is G.

The cost of evaluating a Fourier transform or its inverse is high; the exponential terms only need calculating once, and can thereafter be fetched from a lookup table, but nevertheless equation II.1 involves of the order of MN multiplications for *each* point (u,v), and thus of the order of M^2N^2 multiplications to compute the whole transform. In recognition of this, a number of short cuts in evaluating transforms have evolved; notable among these is the *Fast Fourier Transform* always abbreviated *FFT*. The FFT makes some assumptions about the image dimensions being highly composite, and preferably of the form $N=2^n$, $M=2^m$ for some m and n; it then turns out to be possible to compute the transform with order $M\log_2 MN\log_2 N$ multiplications, which represents a considerable saving. Any reference on Fourier theory will provide the details.

Filters

There are many Image Processing software libraries; just one example is (Spider 1983). All such libraries will include optimally coded routines to perform Fourier and other transforms. Strictly speaking, this means that the details of how the transform is calculated are not essential knowledge - what it is necessary to know is why the transform is calculated in the first place, and what the associated filters are trying to achieve. As outlined in Chapter 4, the variables of the transformed function can be interpreted as *frequencies* present in the original function. In the context of an image, high frequencies will indicate sharp changes in intensity (e.g. edges) and low frequencies will represent areas of low contrast (e.g. region interiors). Fourier filters are applied to the transformed function to emphasise some frequencies and damp down others; an example Fourier filter to accentuate high frequencies would involve forming the function

$$H(u,v) = 0 \quad \text{if } \sqrt{u^2+v^2}<R$$

$= 1$ *otherwise*

for some R. Now if $T(f(x,y))=F(u,v)$, the function $H(u,v)F(u,v)$ selects out the higher frequencies present in the transformed function. Applying the inverse transform to this function product should yield an image with its high frequencies enhanced; Figure 4.8 shows an example of applying just this sort of filter with radius $R=1.0$. Observe that the edges are indeed enhanced, but the low frequencies areas (region interiors) are attenuated as a result of their contribution in transform space being filtered out.

This is just one very crude example of the Fourier filtering technique - there are many different and better ways of achieving similar effects, just as there are many transforms other than the Fourier transform. The interested reader is referred to a more specialised text.

APPENDIX III

Clowes´ Line Labelling

The table that follows should be read in conjunction with Chapter 7; it lists the possible 3D interpretations of 2D junctions. This table is taken from (Clowes 1971) which is happily acknowledged here - the terminology is fully explained in the Chapter and the original reference.

Notice from the table that

(1)   One of the TEE junctions is a limiting case of an ARROW junction, so they are both of Type 1.

(2)   The other TEE junctions are all caused by occlusion, and therefore do not correspond to 3D junctions at all.

(3)   The INVISIBLE junctions of a given Type (*I*, *II*, *III* or *IV*) cannot sensibly be distinguished from one another as they appear in a 2D picture.

Table III.1

Picture Type	Scene Type	Canonical Number	Scene Fragment		
ARROW	I_2	1	vx(B',X',a')	vx(B',C',b')	vx(C',X',c')
			hind(B',A',a')		hind(C',A',c')
ARROW	II_3	2	vx(A',B',a')	cv(B',C',b')	vx(A',C',c')
ARROW	III_3	3	cv(A',B',a')	vx(B',C',b')	cv(A',C',c')
ELL	I_1	4	vx(B',X',a')	vx(B',Y',b')	vx(X',Y',x')
			hind(B',A',a')	hind(B',A',b')	
ELL	II_1	5	vx(A',X',a')	vx(A',Y',b')	cv(X',Y',x')
			hind(A',B',a')	hind(A',B',b')	
ELL	II_2	6	vx(A',B',a')	vx(A',X',b')	cv(B',X',x')
				hind(A',B',b')	
ELL	II_2	7	vx(A',X',a')	vx(A',B',b')	cv(B',X',x')
			hind(A',B',a')		
ELL	III_2	8	cv(A',B',a')	vx(B',X',b')	cv(A',X',x')
				hind(B',A',b')	
ELL	III_2	9	vx(B',X',a')	cv(B',A',b')	cv(A',X',x')
			hind(B',A',a')		
FORK	I_3	10	vx(A',B',a')	vx(B',C',b')	vx(C',A',c')
FORK	IV_3	11	cv(A',B',a')	cv(B',C',b')	cv(C',A',c')
FORK	II_2	12	vx(B',X',a')	cv(B',C',b')	vx(C',X',c')
			hind(B',A',a')		hind(C',A',c')
FORK	II_2	13	vx(A',X',a')	vx(C',X',b')	cv(A',C',c')
			hind(A',B',a')	hind(C',B',b')	
FORK	II_2	14	cv(A',B',a')	vx(B',X',b')	vx(A',X',c')
				hind(B',C',b')	hind(A',C',c')
TEE	I_2	1	vx(B',X',a')	vx(B',C',b')	vx(C',X',c')
			hind(B',A',a')		hind(C',A',c')
TEE	-	15	vx(A',X',a')	vx(B',Y',b')	vx(A',X',c')
			hind(A',B',a')	hind(B',C',b')	hind(A',C',c')
TEE	-	16	vx(A',X',a')	vx(B',C',b')	vx(A',X',c')
			hind(A',B',a')		hind(A',C',c')
TEE	-	17	vx(A',X',a')	vx(C',Y',b')	vx(A',X',c')
			hind(A',B',a')	hind(C',B',b')	hind(A',C',c')
TEE	-	18	vx(A',X',a')	cv(B',C',b')	vx(A',X',c')
			hind(A',B',a')		hind(A',C',c')
INVISIBLE	I_0	19	vx(X',Y',x')	vx(Y',Z',y')	vx(Z',X',z')
INVISIBLE	II_0	20	vx(X',Y',x')	vx(Y',Z',y')	cv(Z',X',z')
--------------	-------	-----------	----------------	----------------	----------------
INVISIBLE	III_0 III_1	21	vx(X',Y',x')	cv(Y',Z',y')	cv(Z',X',z')
--------------	-------	-----------	----------------	----------------	----------------
INVISIBLE	IV_0 IV_1 IV_2	22	cv(X',Y',x')	cv(Y',Z',y')	cv(Z',X',z')

Goad's Vision Algorithm

Introduction

In this Appendix we describe the operation of a particular model based Vision algorithm due to Christopher Goad of Stanford University, California, USA (Goad 1983). Goad's algorithm is interesting since it is simple enough in principle to show how the task may be done, but generates enough complexities in implementation to illustrate how difficult Vision can become. In fact, Goad's work was not principally aimed at solving a Vision problem but was a demonstration of a particular technique - special purpose automatic programming.

Goad's algorithm aims to locate the 3D co-ordinates *and* orientation of a known object from a single intensity image; the object is "known" in the sense that its edges (which we assume to be straight), and their relative position to each other, are exhaustively listed in the model of the object that we have; there will be no ambiguity in the model about visibility, such as a wire frame may cause (see Chapter 8). Following the terminology of the original reference, in this Appendix an *object edge* will refer to a straight line segment in three-space that forms part of the boundary of an object face. Projections of these into two space (the image) are referred to as *lines*.

The strategy is not to extract 3D (depth) information from the single image, but rather to search for a projection of the object which matches the lines detected in it. The details described here focus on the matching technique used, and not the edge/boundary/line detection - it is assumed that an edge and line detector has done its work and we have extracted the lines (straight boundaries) in the image. The algorithm permits these extracted lines to be imprecise within certain bounds, and, in its full form, is able to make allowances for spurious and missing evidence (that is, lines where there should be none and no lines where there should be).

The specific characteristic of this algorithm is that it attempts 3D Vision from an exact model. This contrasts with the "pseudo 2D" problem of locating an object of known, or near known, orientation (which is relatively easier) or the more difficult problem of locating generally positioned objects whose precise description is not fully known. It may be argued that the first of these is a more realistic problem in industrial situations - in the factory *some* foreknowledge about orientation is very likely. A solution to the latter would have much more important consequences in that there are many more applications in which it may be useful. Goad's algorithm has been demonstrated to work, however, and may therefore be argued to be interesting in its own right.

The General Strategy

The idea of the algorithm is intuitively simple. We take an edge of the object and find a likely match for it in the image. This possible match will not constrain the position of the object completely - there will be a range (a *locus*) of camera positions that is consistent with what is observed. Now select another edge from the model; the restrictions provided by the (putatively) matched edge will limit the possible position of the projection of this new edge into the image; we may thus *predict* the position of this edge in the image, within bounds governed by the accuracy of measurements and line finders. If this projected edge cannot be located, the supposed match is false. If it can, we hope it restricts the locus of possible camera positions that is consistent with all hitherto deduced possible camera positions - the *observation* is used to *back project* and thereby reduce the possible locus. Another edge is now selected and the procedure repeated iteratively until either the match fails, or we have strong enough evidence (enough matched edges, and a restricted enough locus) to deduce that the match is correct and thereby specify the object's location and orientation. Early in the matching process, with few object edges matched, the bounds on the prediction may be very wide; as the match proceeds so the predictions will become more precise. When the match fails, we may backtrack to a point where more than one image edge was a possible match for an object edge and try again.

This Predict-Observe-Back Project cycle is a simple instantiation of an elementary matching algorithm - sequential matching with backtracking (Hayes Roth et al., 1983).

Assumptions

The implementation scheme makes some assumptions about the object and the camera viewing positions. We have already remarked that the object boundaries shall be straight edges. We further assume

(1) The object to be located is either fully in the field of view, or not visible at all.
(2) The distance to the object is known; this permits us to assume that the camera lies at some point on a sphere centred at the origin of an

object-based co-ordinate system. Without loss of generality, we assume this is a unit sphere.

(3)   The field of view is sufficiently narrow to permit us to assume that changing the *orientation* of the camera at a given position only causes the features in view to undergo a simple rotation and translation. While such a change in orientation may affect which features are visible, the lengths of lines in view will not alter, within a small tolerance.

Notation and Definitions

Remember we are working in object-centred co-ordinates, so the object is regarded as fixed while the camera position and orientation are the unknowns to be determined. Throughout, an object edge will be regarded as an *oriented* line segment, given by an ordered pair of co-ordinates, while an image line may be unoriented. Thus an object edge is an *ordered* pair of (3D) co-ordinates, while an image line is given by a (perhaps unordered) pair of (2D) co-ordinates.

Let p be a 3D (camera) position, and q a 3D (camera) orientation. p is just a 3D co-ordinate, which we are constraining to lie on the unit sphere. If e is an object edge, let $P([p,q],e)$ denote the *oriented* image line which results from viewing e from p at orientation q, using an ordinary perspective transformation (Foley & Van Dam, 1982). $P([p,q],e)$ may be undefined if e is occluded, or the projection is outside the field of view. If it is defined, it is an *ordered* pair of 2D co-ordinates.

There will be a finite number of possible camera positions on the unit sphere - Goad suggested drawing a 6x6 grid on each face of a cube, and radially projecting this onto the sphere surface, giving a total of 216 possible camera positions. (If this figure seems a little strange, note that the work was done on a PDP-10[*] with a 36 bit word. This permits the whole ''sphere'' (or any locus) to be stored as a bit map in 6 machine words; operations on loci (mainly intersections) may then be performed very fast. Of course, other divisions of the sphere surface may be chosen to suit other architectures.) A set of such positions will be referred to as a *locus*. A given edge e will only be visible from some of these positions, which we will refer to as the *visibility locus* of e.

An assignment M between object edges and images lines will be called a *match*. For an object edge e, $M(e)$ will denote the oriented image line assigned to it by M; for some e, $M(e)$ may be undefined, so a match need not be a complete assignment of object edges. Then a match M is consistent with a camera position and orientation $[p,q]$ if for each object edge e we

---

[*]PDP-10 is a trademark of the Digital Equipment Corporation.

have $P([p,q],e) \approx M(e)$ to within errors of measurement. A match M is consistent with a camera position p if there is some orientation q such that M is consistent with $[p,q]$. A match is consistent with a locus L if it is consistent with every position of that locus. L is initialised from the assumptions deduced from the match of the first edge.

Algorithm Overview

We assume we have at least one edge (putatively) matched. (The first edge to be matched must be tried at all plausible positions). Suppose M is the current match and L is the current locus; an unmatched edge e is selected. By considering a particular matched edge e_0, we can compute bounds for the possible position of $P([p,q],e)$ relative to $P([p,q],e_0)$ as p ranges over L - remember assumption 3 above tells us that the relative position of e and e_0 depends only on p and not on q. These bounds will define a range of positions in the image in which $M(e)$ (if it exists) must lie. e_0 will probably be a fixed reference edge that we assume will be matched early in the process.

If we do not find a candidate for $M(e)$, the algorithm must at this point backtrack; if we find more than one candidate then this represents a choice point in the algorithm for any future necessary backtracking. Having found a candidate for $M(e)$ we now *back project* - that is, restrict the locus L to L' by rejecting all points in L that are not consistent with the measured position of $M(e)$. L' is simply those points p in L from which the predicted position of $P([p,q],e)$ relative to $P([p,q],e_0)$ is the same as the position of $M(e)$ relative to $M(e_0)$, to within measurement error.

Imperfections in the Line Detector

We have to acknowledge that the image line detector is not going to be perfect; we have observed many times that lighting and noise effects will combine to cause discontinuities in, or absence of, some lines, while some spurious evidence may be expected to occur. This we do by admitting that some e, although expected to be in view, will not have a match $M(e)$ in the image. What is necessary is to determine some probabilities that allow us to quantify whether a match is proceeding plausibly. We will tolerate a small number of unmatched edges, but when the probability of the accumulated mismatches falls below a certain threshold, we abandon the match and backtrack, deducing that the match is at fault rather than the line detector.

More precisely, we maintain two measures as the match proceeds;
Reliability

We compute the probability that the edges making up the match to date arose by chance from background information. The inverse of the probability we call the *reliability* of the match. When the reliability exceeds a certain threshold, we regard the match as correct and terminate the algorithm. These probabilities may best be computed on the basis of statistics gathered from images of the same class as that under examination.

Plausibility

Assuming the match is correct, and has missed some edges, we compute the probability that those edges would indeed have been missed by the line detector in use - these probabilities assume knowledge of the performance of the line detector which once again are best accumulated from running it on sample images.

Now high reliability indicates that the match is correct, while low plausibility indicates it is probably incorrect (although we must beware - high plausibility does not imply a correct match and low reliability does not imply it is incorrect: The reader may care to explain why).

We introduce plausibility into the algorithm by requiring that if it falls below a certain threshold, then we must backtrack. In fact, we have generated another possible choice point - if we assume e is visible, search for it and fail to find it, we will assume it should be visible but is absent from the image and proceed with reduced plausibility accordingly. Only if this assumption leads to no match do we backtrack to consider edge visibility (below).

Visibility

When we select the next edge e for matching we consider first whether e is actually visible from the points of L (that is, whether V, the visibility locus of e, intersects L). We have here another possible choice point for backtracking; we first assume e is visible (that is, restrict L to its intersection with V) and proceed as described above. If we fail to find a match and require to backtrack, at this point we can now assume e is not visible and restrict L to its intersection with the complement of V.

"Visibility" needs to be defined with caution here - we only regard an edge as visible if it is likely to be found by the line detector. Very short lines (object edges viewed nearly "end on" for instance) would not meet this criterion.

"Compile Time" Efficiency

A feature of the problem that this algorithm is designed to solve is that the object we search for is modelled *precisely*. We can exploit this fact to speed up what would otherwise be at best a ponderous execution by going through a "set up" phase during which the features of the object are coded into the algorithm to be exploited at run time. Goad refers to this as the "compile time" of the algorithm.

There are several ways we may exploit this compile time;

(1)   From a given position p, we require during the algorithm to determine bounds on the position of an edge e relative to a matched edge e_0. This relative position, $relpos(e,e_0,p)$ depends only on the object, which is fully characterised independent of the run. These relative position bounds may therefore be computed at compile time and stored for lookup.

In fact we require $relpos(e,e_0,p)$ for all $p \varepsilon L$; this is easily done by taking the union of the bounds for each such p.

This table can also be used for the back projection; given a likely $M(e)$ we need only determine for which $p \varepsilon L$ this $M(e)$ is within the bounds predicted by $relpos(e,e_0,p)$.

(2)   When selecting the next edge to match, care should be taken that we maximise the return on the effort put into trying to match it. We do this by ensuring that the likelihood of the selected edge being visible (and findable by the line detector) is as high as possible and by requiring that the measurements of the image position of the observed edge should provide as much information as possible about the camera position (so the locus is reduced as much as possible by making a match).

We can make these judgements at compile time. Suppose we assume a uniform distribution of camera positions around the sphere (in fact, allowances can be made if this is an unreasonable assumption) then the probability of the visibility of a given edge over any locus can be precomputed. Likewise, the "value" of measuring the position of a given edge can be computed at compile time. If we determine a way of combining these factors by appropriately weighting the values determined (and this is not necessarily straightforward), the "best next edge" to match, given a particular partial match, can be determined at compile time. Goad admits that this particular precomputation may be very expensive.

(3)   The elemental contributions to the plausibility measurements can also be precomputed.

There is no doubt that performing the compile time operations outlined will be very expensive, but this should not worry us since the expected run time efficiency gain will make the effort well worth the cost. It is a familiar idea to pay the price of lengthy compilation in order to generate efficient running code.

Remarks

Goad's algorithm is in principle quite simple - there is a variety of things we may expect to see, and we search for them in a 2D projection. Nevertheless, when examined with all its ramifications, it should be clear that the algorithm's implementation is not quite so simple.

When running, Goad managed to get respectable efficiency from his system. To deduce a complete match, it is really only necessary to make reliable matches for four object edges. He reports that on an "average 1 MIP machine" [Goad refers to the PDP-10, Motorola 68000 and VAX* (probably 750 or 780) - remember this work is dated 1983], one matching step will take of the order of a few milliseconds, permitting several hundred attempts at matching every second. The runtime for a complete match is quoted at approximately one second, but this excludes edge and line detection. As has been remarked, much of this efficiency has been achieved at the expense of a very long "compile time".

The algorithm has actually been applied to several problems - single occurrences of objects such as a connecting rod or universal joint have been located in cluttered scenes, and, more interesting, key caps (the plastic keys from a keyboard or typewriter) have been located in an image of a pile of caps. In industrial terms this problem, often referred to as *bin picking*, is unreasonably difficult - multiple occurrences of the target object at multiple orientations, many partially occluded (remember the first assumption above, that the object is visible either fully or not at all). The algorithm succeeds despite the fact that the background consists of features very similar to those composing the target, and that the target has few distinguishing features.

Goad's algorithm turns out to be quite powerful. The idea of "precompiling" the object description (special purpose automatic programming) produces systems of acceptable efficiency. Various elaborations exist which we will not explore here, such as exploiting recurring patterns or symmetries in the object, or variable camera-to-object distance. Remember this object location is done by two dimensional matching; that it works despite unknown orientation is dependent on complete and thorough knowledge of the image and line detector properties, and the target object.

---

*VAX is a trademark of the Digital Equipment Corporation.

APPENDIX V

Solutions to Exercises

Solutions are presented here to those exercises for which they are appropriate. They vary in detail, but where a full solution is not provided, a reference is given where the topic in question may be further explored.

Chapter 1

Exercise 1.1

The list of examples may be as long or as short as you please, but notice that *recognition* may well be a sub-problem of assembly and inspection, both of which are common industrial Vision applications. It is also the case that assembly and inspection will probably require the Vision system to locate specific objects with accuracy - that is, their position and orientation in three-space; for the former this will be preparatory to manipulating the object, for the latter so that the inspection process can be sure of the component with which it is comparing its "ideal".

Navigation (a mobile robot, for example) does not of course require actual recognition of obstacles, only the ability to see that they are there. This does not make the problem any easier; navigating robots must maintain a coherent idea of the *perspective* of what they see, since obstacles may appear at any distance. The robot must distinguish between an elephant at 10 yards and a chair at three feet. In the industrial arena, there is likely to be much closer control over, and foreknowledge of, object-camera distance.

Chapter 2

Exercise 2.1

The patterns score as shown in Table V.1. As we might expect, the AND test is strict, giving a positive score if and only if the "normal" score was 3. The OR test is very mild, giving a positive result if the normal test scores more than 0.

Exercise 2.2

The enumeration of maximum scoring patterns is straightforward; each

177

Table V.1

	Normal	AND	OR
1	1	0	1
2	1	0	1
3	3	1	1

RAM has a 1 at two of its addresses, giving a total of $2^3=8$ such patterns, including the teaching set.

Reconnecting so that RAM 1 takes its address from column 1 (and so on), the teaching set in the text would give RAM contents thus:

Table V.2

	0	1	2	3	4	5	6	7
RAM 1	0	0	0	0	1	0	0	0
RAM 2	0	0	0	0	0	0	1	1
RAM 3	0	0	1	0	1	0	0	0

The maximum scoring set is the teaching set and the "T" shown in Figure V.1.

1	1	0
0	1	1
0	0	0

Figure V.1 A maximum scoring pattern

Exercise 2.3

Recall that each RAM has a 1 at two of its addresses. For case *(i)* we need to generate a "score" of 2, so there will be 3x2x2x6=72 ways of doing this. In case *(ii)* the maximum score is 4, and we can only generate a score of 3 by getting a 1 response from RAM 1. The total number of ways is thus 2x2x2x6=48.

What is instructive in this example is that these "one offs" are arguably more "T" like than many of those from the unweighted discriminator. This is because we have added more weight to the RAM that selects one of the important (to us) characteristics of the "T", its horizontal bar. We could have tuned a discriminator to the vertical bar by using a vertical RAM allocation (as in question 2.2) and weighting the second column. WISARD, with its random allocation of bits to RAMs, does not exploit this kind of tuning.

Chapter 3

Exercise 3.1

A general rule of equipment procurement is that whatever you get, the user complains. Nevertheless, in a general purpose laboratory, one might hope for equipment that would be useful in as many areas as possible. It would therefore have a large variety of software available, and the facility to develop more. Hardware reliability and extendibility would be important, with a clearly defined upgrade path as enhancements became available.

A navigation system on the other hand would probably regard weight as an important criterion and, above all, speed. The aim must be to achieve real time analysis of the scene in view so that the robot's movement suffers mechanical constraints rather than computational ones.

In a manufacturing environment the prime requirement is reliability. The Vision system only has one task to perform so (in relative terms) need not be too elaborate. Industrial atmospheres are often oil and dirt filled, so rugged apparatus too would be a necessity.

Exercise 3.2

We may co-ordinatise this tessellation by counting rows vertically, then triangles along a row (so pixel (x,y) will be x triangles along the yth row from the top). An obvious problem for this tessellation is the boundaries, where "half triangles" will appear. We can use the ordinary Euclidean metric, or that given in equation 3.1, but a problem is that "x" distance is not the same as "y" distance - that is, two pixels differing in their x co-ordinates by a quantity d are not going to be the same *physical* distance apart as two pixels differing by d in their y co-ordinates.

Exercise 3.3

(i) Such a disc is a (digitised) circle of radius r.

(ii) The disc becomes a "diamond" (a square with its diagonal vertical). The diagonal length will be $2r$.

(iii) Figure V.2 shows the disc $d(\mathbf{a},\mathbf{x}) \leq 4$ for the Euclidean metric.

Figure V.2 A triangular tessellation disc

Exercise 3.4

Run length encoding comes in various flavours, and will be well explained in any standard Image Processing text. A simple scheme is to map each image row to a series of integer pairs

$$(n_1, g_1), (n_2, g_2), \dots (n_r, g_r)$$

denoting n_1 pixels of intensity g_1, followed by n_2 pixels of intensity g_2 an so on. If the image has N_1 pixels per row, and N_2 rows, clearly

$$N_1 = \sum_{i=1}^{r} g_i$$

and the minimum space the encoded image can consume is $2 \times N_2$ integers. A slight elaboration is to allow the end of one row to wrap to the beginning of the next, thereby allowing large bands of uniform intensity to be encoded even more efficiently.

"Live" systems will not use run length encoding since the image data is inaccessible, at least in the form that we may want it (although (Kahan et al., 1987) provides an interesting counterexample in the area of character recognition). For instance, knowing that pixel (i, j) is of a particular intensity, we may well want to know the intensities of the pixels directly above and below; these are not immediately available.

Exercise 3.5

Many applications depend on or can heavily exploit colour. Some examples are resistor classification (resistors are colour coded), "automatic cartography" (rivers are blue, roads are red ...) and automatic fruit inspection. This last may be easy with, for example, oranges but much harder with apples - a ripe apple may have several colours (red, green, yellow ...) whose segmentation may be confused with bruising. Likewise the stalk can become confused with wormholes.

A survey of these problems can be found in (Thomas & Connolly, 1986).

Chapter 4

Exercise 4.1

Algorithms that perform, e.g., median filtering or K-closest averaging are notoriously slow since they must sort the window contents at each pixel position; how efficient your solution is depends on how much thought you have given to overcoming this. The best that can be done is to note that after the computation of an average, the window may, for instance, be slid right one pixel for the next computation. Its contents are now partially known from its last position, and this can be used to reduce the sort load, but it needs an agile mind to do this optimally.

Exercise 4.2

Suppose the noise "function", $q(i,j)$ is uniformly distributed in the range $[0,+n]$. Then the pixel at (i,j) will be corrupted to grey level $f'(i,j)$ thus;

$$f'(i,j) = f(i,j)+q(i,j)$$

(subject to maximum grey level constraints). Then, for a window $W(i,j)$ centred on (i,j) we have

$$\sum_{(k,l)\varepsilon W(i,j)} f'(k,l) = \sum_{(k,l)\varepsilon W(i,j)} f(k,l) + \sum_{(k,l)\varepsilon W(i,j)} q(k,l)$$

and the expectation value of the second (noise) term is $\dfrac{|W|n}{2}$ (if the noise had been uniformly distributed about 0, this expectation would have been 0). We might therefore write

$$f^*(i,j) = \frac{1}{n}(\sum_{(k,l)\varepsilon W(i,j)} f'(k,l) - \frac{|W|}{2})$$

(taking care that $f^*(i,j) >= 0$), and hope that f^* is a "cleaner" image. This makes all the usual assumptions about the window having "even" contrast, and there will be blurring of edges as with the usual mean filters.

Exercise 4.4

The histograms have the shapes shown in Figure V.3. The first aims to produce a higher number of light pixels than dark. The second is a "distorted" equalisation with the extremes damped in favour of the "middle of the range".

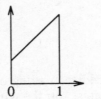 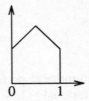

Figure V.3 Probability density functions

Deriving these transforms is not difficult - one way is to determine the transform required to equalise the *destination* histogram (T_1 say). Then if T_2 is the transformation that equalises the image histogram, $T_1^{-1}(T_2)$ will transform the image histogram to that desired. T_1^{-1} may not be well defined, but interpolation solves this problem. Such techniques are described thoroughly in (Gonzalez & Wintz, 1987).

Exercise 4.6

Simple templates may be extensions of the Sobel operator idea, perhaps as illustrated in Figure V.4, which will just aim to measure intensity gradient in the horizontal and vertical directions.

1	1	1	1	1
1	1	2	1	1
0	0	0	0	0
-1	-1	-2	-1	-1
-1	-1	-1	-1	-1

-1	-1	0	1	1
-1	-1	0	1	1
-1	-2	0	2	1
-1	-1	0	1	1
-1	-1	0	1	1

Figure V.4 Large edge templates

Given the size of the template, we may look for evidence of oblique lines, or corners, with templates like those shown in Figure V.5. There is a lot of scope now. We can offer up a large number of corner/edge features and test an area of the image for similarity. Such an idea has been tried (Frei & Chen, 1977) with 3x3 templates, attempting to use a large set of difference operators as a set of orthogonal basis functions. The "projection" of the image onto the various basis functions measures its similarity to any one of them.

0	0	-1	-1	0
0	-1	-2	0	1
-1	-2	0	2	1
-1	0	2	1	0
0	1	1	0	0

-1	-1	0	2	1
-1	-1	0	3	2
-1	-2	0	0	0
-1	-3	-2	-1	-1
-1	-1	-1	-1	0

Figure V.5 Corner and diagonal templates

Chapter 5

Exercise 5.1

The histogram shape we hope for is illustrated in Figure V.6. As in the text, we may partition the image and look for bi- or tri-modal behaviour in the sub-images (bimodal since a subimage may not contain both objects). We can then hope to interpolate as necessary.

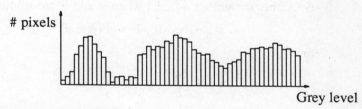

pixels

Grey level

Figure V.6 A trimodal histogram

The problems may be firstly insufficient grey range to distinguish the peaks and troughs, and secondly the peaks may not correspond in different subimages. That is, the grey levels inside the "object" regions may overlap to such an extent that in one subimage one object is the brightest while in another one, the other object is. It is easy to see that such elementary ideas do not generalise well.

Exercise 5.2

The edges within distance two of a given edge's end points are illustrated in Figure V.7. We may categorise (in the manner of Prager) (Prager 1980) by counting the number of boundary segments of length one and of length two incident at each end; the latter lend more evidence of the target edge being on a boundary than the former, so there is scope for different probability increments, depending on the weight of evidence. We may also look for edges at distance two not apparently connected to the target edge. If there were such edges at both ends we might deduce that we were in the neighbourhood of a boundary with low contrast, and adjust probabilities accordingly.

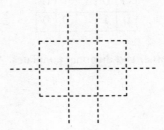

Figure V.7 Edges up to distance 2

Exercise 5.4

If we have some confidence that the edge direction is correct, it might be wise to try a scheme such as (in the notation of the text);

 (i) Doubly increment $A[a,b]$ when a and b are solutions of

$$a = x + R\cos\theta \quad b = y + R\sin\theta \qquad \text{V.1}$$

for

$$|\theta - \phi| \leq \frac{\delta\phi}{2} \quad \text{or} \quad |\theta + \phi| \leq \frac{\delta\phi}{2}$$

(similarly to Equation 5.6)

 (ii) Increment $A[a,b]$ when a and b are solutions of Equation V.1 for

$$\frac{\delta\phi}{2} < |\theta - \phi| \leq \delta\phi \quad \text{or} \quad \frac{\delta\phi}{2} < |\theta + \phi| \leq \delta\phi$$

There are obvious further extensions to this idea, such as making the increment proportional to the edge strength.

Exercise 5.5

This solution is gleaned direct from (Feldman & Yakimovsky, 1974) in which successful practical experiments used the following ideas.

Six "types" of region were defined: sky, road, roadside vegetation, car, shadow of car, tree. Colour images, encoded using the IHS scheme, had these regions categorised into 4 intensity classes, 8 hue classes, 4 saturation classes, 5 size classes (logarithmically scaled), 4 vertical position classes and 4 horizontal position classes.

With six types of region, we have $\dfrac{6\times6}{2}$=18 types of boundary. These boundaries were separated into 6 relative size classes (logarithmically scaled), 6 relative intensity classes (logarithmically scaled), relative colour classes (3 red, 3 green, 3 blue), 21 shape and orientation classes, 16 position classes and 5 classes according to boundary length.

Their results were remarkably successful, managing to identify "grass" even though it appeared as several regions of brown, yellow and grey. The program had difficulty identifying the car correctly, although this was solved by providing clues such as "the car is on the road"; this sort of information is integral to later, similar work (Tenenbaum & Barrow, 1977).

Exercise 5.6

The probability P_f gives the probability of boundary B_{ij} being false; that is, separating two regions of the same interpretation. We can write

$$P_f =$$

$$\sum_p Pr\,(B_{ij} \text{ is between } I_p, I_p \mid \text{ measurements of } B_{ij})\times$$

$$Pr\,(R_i \text{ is } I_p \mid \text{ measurements of } R_i)\times$$

$$Pr\,(R_j \text{ is } I_p \mid \text{ measurements of } R_j)$$

That P_{false} is reasonable is a simple matter of conditional probabilities; we are restricting ourselves to inspecting a small part of the whole, thus we should not view P_f in absolute terms, but in relation to $P_f + P_t$.

Chapter 6

Exercise 6.1

The circles would provide centre evidence just away from the true centre position; the net effect is a (small) ring of evidence centred at the true centre. It is possible to identify this effect and hence pinpoint the centre and true radius.

Exercise 6.2

The circumferences of very small circles are, when digitised, very hard to distinguish from squares and other small polygons. Particularly if we are searching for incomplete circles, we shall get confused by features such as corners.

Chapter 7

Exercise 7.2

Since (in the notation of Chapter 7) all junctions are of Type *I*, Table 7.2 simplifies to tell us that an ELL is a junction with one face visible, a FORK is a junction with three faces visible, and an ARROW and TEE both represent a junction with two faces visible. (INVISIBLE junctions can have no visible faces.)

The restriction of Table III.1 also has precisely one possible interpretation for each picture junction type, together with the TEE "occlusion" junctions. Such a restricted world would obviously be much simpler to analyse than a general block world. It need not be regarded as totally unrealistic - there are a lot of convex polyhedra about.

Exercise 7.3

Notice that the "interior" ELL vertex (the one with a line missing in the 3D interpretation) must have one of $hind(A',B',a')$, $hind(A',B',b')$, $hind(B',A',a')$, $hind(B',A',b')$. (That is, one arm of the ELL is occluding). This line is simultaneously the central arm of an ARROW, and there is no ARROW interpretation that has an occluding central arm. This contradiction tells us the figure has no corresponding 3-space body.

Simple extensions to the algorithm may be to *assume* that the large surrounding region is background, and interpolate edges wherever possible, looking for a valid solid. This would not take too long since missing edges can only join vertices at which just two edges meet already.

More intelligent (and interesting) would be to notice that the Figure has two parallel lines, and that there is an obvious position for another parallel one to be introduced. This introduction would complete the solid. Exploitation of features such as parallel boundaries can be a powerful technique (Lowe 1985).

Exercise 7.4

If a point is at the origin of gradient space, it represents a plane of the form

$$a_z z + 1 = 0$$

- that is, parallel to the image plane. The further a point is from the origin of gradient space, the steeper its corresponding plane is inclined to the image plane.

Consider two planes in 3-space,

$$a_x x + a_y y + a_z z + 1 = 0$$

and

$$b_x x + b_y y + b_z z + 1 = 0$$

Simple substitution tells us that the projection of their intersection onto the image plane ($z = 0$) is the line

$$(a_x b_z - a_z b_x)x + (a_y b_z - a_z b_y)y + (b_z - a_z) = 0$$

whose gradient is

$$-\frac{(a_x b_z - a_z b_x)}{(a_y b_z - a_z b_y)}$$

Meanwhile in gradient space the planes are represented by the points $(\frac{a_x}{a_z}, \frac{a_y}{a_z})$ and $(\frac{b_x}{b_z}, \frac{b_y}{b_z})$. The gradient of the line joining these two is

$$\frac{(a_z b_y - a_y b_z)}{(a_z b_x - a_x b_z)}$$

That is, normal to the line in the image plane if we overlay the planes as suggested. This constraint is at the heart of Mackworth's algorithm (Mackworth 1973).

Chapter 8

Exercise 8.1

We know that

$$f(x + \delta x, y + \delta y, t + \delta t) = f(x, y, t)$$

and a Taylor expansion gives

$$f(x + \delta x, y + \delta y, t + \delta t) =$$

$$f(x, y, t) + \delta x \frac{\partial f}{\partial x} + \delta y \frac{\partial f}{\partial y} + \delta t \frac{\partial f}{\partial t} + O(\delta^2)$$

truncating the expansion and substituting gives

$$\delta x \frac{\partial f}{\partial x} + \delta y \frac{\partial f}{\partial y} + \delta t \frac{\partial f}{\partial t} \approx 0$$

Whence

$$-\frac{\partial f}{\partial t} \approx \frac{\partial f}{\partial x}\frac{dx}{dt} + \frac{\partial f}{\partial y}\frac{dy}{dt}$$

In this equation the *partial* derivatives may all be calculated (or at least estimated) from the image sequence, leaving a linear equation relating $\frac{dx}{dt}$ and $\frac{dy}{dt}$, the quantities we wish to know.

Exercise 8.2

A simple matter of co-ordinate geometry; a given light point in the image defines a line (from itself through the focal point) in three space along which the point off which it reflects may lie; this point in three space must also intersect the light plane. If the focal point is already in the light plane, so then is the whole line and we do not have a solitary intersection point as required.

Exercise 8.3

Less likely, but equally admissible, is the interpretation of the *vertical* row of four matches in Figure 8.4 being correct. Imagine a line perpendicularly bisecting the line joining the cameras (or eyes), and place four points on this line. They are all at different disparity, and have the interesting property that the leftmost in the left image is the rightmost in the right image (and vice versa).

This interpretation does not violate the first constraint exploited by the Marr Poggio algorithm (one point matches at most one point) but does violate the second (disparities are "close"). The algorithm behaves as in fact our brains will; on the basis of the stereo evidence alone, it seems more likely that the points are in a horizontal line of equal disparity than on a "receding" line.

Exercise 8.4

With the quoted parameters, isolated points would not match anything since the threshold can only be reached as a result of reinforcement from the excitatory neighbourhood. This seems reasonable - our brains cannot match completely isolated points; we need some "local encouragement" to believe any conclusion.

Indeed, the analysis of this algorithm (Marr et al., 1978) states that with the indicated values;

.. a pattern of five connected points is the smallest configuration that can survive. It will not grow unless one other point is added.

Chapter 9

Exercise 9.1

A very simple description of a dinner plate would consist of a cylinder with a length very much shorter than its diameter. Thus, assuming dimensions are in centimetres, we could have:

Node: DINNER_PLATE

CLASS:	SIMPLE_CONE
SPINE:	STRAIGHT_LENGTH_1
SWEEPING_RULE:	CONSTANT
CROSS_SECTION:	CIRCLE_RADIUS_12

The cutlery requires a bigger leap in the imagination, but a bar with square cross section would suffice.

Node: GENERIC_CUTLERY

CLASS:	SIMPLE_CONE
SPINE:	$17 \leq$ STRAIGHT_LENGTH ≤ 22
SWEEPING_RULE:	CONSTANT
CROSS_SECTION:	SQUARE_SIDE_1

The table top can be created either by sweeping the top down through the thickness of the top, or its side can be swept along the table length. We show below the former.

Node: TABLE-TOP

CLASS:	SIMPLE_CONE
SPINE:	STRAIGHT_LENGTH_3
SWEEPING_RULE:	CONSTANT
CROSS_SECTION:	SQUARE_SIDE_120

Exercise 9.2

We can say that a fork consists of a set of prongs attached to a handle. In order to complete the description we would need to be able to define the number of prongs and the required rotation and translation to attach them to the handle. In ACRONYM terms we would need to use affixment frames (Brooks 1981) to store the geometric transformations.

Exercise 9.3

The letter "I" might match the right hand side of the "H" and perhaps the "N" if the dimensions were not too closely checked. More contextual information would be required to remove the ambiguities. For example the left hand side of the "H" would be left un-matched in the "I" case, so we would discard it in favour of the "H".

Chapter 10

Exercise 10.1

The general equation of a straight line if $y=mx+c$; the six straight line that interest us may therefore be written

$$V_1: y=m_1x+c_1$$
$$V_2: y=m_2x+c_2$$
$$O_1: y=m_3x+c_3$$
$$O_2: y=m_4x+c_4$$
$$O_3: y=m_5x+c_5$$
$$O_4: y=m_6x+c_6$$

Then the constraints

$$y \leq m_1x+c_1$$
$$y \geq m_2x+c_2$$

define the field of view, while the constraints

$$y \leq m_3x+c_3$$
$$y \leq m_4x+c_4$$
$$y \geq m_5x+c_5$$
$$y \geq m_6x+c_6$$

define the object.

If for a given point *all* the constraints are satisfied, then the object is at least partially visible; to ensure that the object is totally visible we must determine that the object corners, defined by the intersections of line O_1 and O_2 etc., are visible.

Exercise 10.2

An informal procedure might be as follows. First create the "ribbons"; for the plates there are two, a circle corresponding to the plan view and a rectangle corresponding to the side (these are very generous interpretations of "ribbons"). The cutlery becomes basically a pair of parallel lines. Now tranform to allow for viewing position giving an ellipse for the plate. Scale and match. The larger plates would match but not the smaller ones if the scaling is correct. Some of the pieces of cutlery shows very clear parallel lines in their handles. The table legs might get included as candidates for cutlery as well!

Exercise 10.3

Informally we know that the table has longish straight boundaries associated with it. The question is how to decide whether some of the longer straight boundaries in Figure 4.13 are due to the table. The clues come from from consideration of the regions on either side of the boundaries. The region around the chair suggests that the long boundary is continuous; we therefore have an estimate of its length, which we know to be longer than the largest side of the patterned cloth. The far side of the table can likely be locked into the already identified side, and from the size of the top, we can estimate where the near side or "invisible" edge would be.

An alternative line of reasoning is to consider the near part of the cloth which has a region of the same intensity, but the boundary with the next piece of cloth has a bend in it, suggesting the cloth is hanging over the edge of something. This approach requires a fair amount of domain knowledge.

References

G Adorni, L Massone, G Sandini, and E Trucco, Reasoning about iconic data in artificial vision, *Proceedings of the Society of Photo-Optical Instrumentation Engineers* **595** (**Computer Vision for Robots**) pp. 245-255 (1985).

G Adorni, L Massone, G Sandini, and M Immovilli, From early processing to conceptual reasoning: an attempt to fill the gap, pp. 775-778 in *Proceedings 10th Int. Joint Conference on Artificial Intelligence.* IJCAI (1987).

A V Aho, R Sethi, and J D Ullman, *Compilers: Principles, Techniques and Tools*, Addison Wesley, Reading, Massachusetts (1986).

I Aleksander and T J Stonham, Guide to Pattern Recognition using Random Access Memories, *Computers and Digital Techniques* **2**(1) pp. 29-40 (February 1979).

I Aleksander, W V Thomas, and P A Bowden, WISARD - A radical step forward in Image Recognition, pp. 120-124 in *Sensor Review.* (July 1984).

A P Ambler, H G Barrow, C M Brown, R M Burstall, and R J Popplestone, A Versatile Computer-Controlled Assembly System, *Artificial Intelligence* **6**(2) pp. 129-156 (1975).

Armstrong, *NONAME User manual*, GMP, University of Leeds, Leeds, UK (1982).

E S Atwell and S J Elliot, Dealing with Grammatically Ill-formed English Text, in *The Computational Analysis of English.* Ed. R Garride, G Sampson & G Leech, Longman, Harlow, England (1987).

D H Ballard and C M Brown, *Computer Vision*, Prentice Hall, New Jersey (1982).

S T Barnard and W B Thompson, Disparity Analysis of Images, University of Minnesota, Institute of Technology, TR 79-1, University of Minnesota (1979).

B G Batchelor, Image Processing System Design, in *Automated Visual Inspection.* Ed. D C Hodgson, I F S (Publications) Ltd, Bedford UK (1985).

P J Besl and R C Jain, Three-Dimensional Object Recognition, *ACM Computing Surveys* **17**(1) pp. 75-145 (March 1985).

T O Binford, Visual Perception by Computer, in *Proceedings of the IEEE Conference on Systems Science and Cybernetics (Miami).* , Miami (December 1971).

L Bolc (Editor), *Natural Language Communication with Pictorial Information Systems*, Springer-Verlag, Berlin (1984).

192

C Brice and C Fennema, Scene Analysis using Regions, *Artificial Intelligence* **1**(3) pp. 205-226 (1970).

R A Brooks, R Greiner, and T O Binford, The ACRONYM Model-Based Vision System, pp. 105-113 in *Proceedings 6th Int. Joint Conference on Artificial Intelligence.* IJCAI (August 1979).

R A Brooks, Symbolic Reasoning Among 3-D Models and 2-D Images, *Artificial Intelligence* **17** pp. 285-348 (1981).

R A Brooks, Model-based Interpretations of Two-Dimensional Images, *IEEE Transactions on Pattern Analysis and Machine Intelligence* **5**(2) pp. 140-149 (March 1983).

V Bryant, *Metric Spaces*, Cambridge University Press, Cambridge (1985).

J B Burns and L J Kitchen, Recognition in 2D images of 3D objects from large model bases using prediction hierarchies, pp. 763-766 in *Proceedings 10th Int. Joint Conference on Artificial Intelligence.* IJCAI (1987).

J Canny, A Computational Approach to Edge Detection, *IEEE Transactions on Pattern Analysis and Machine Intelligence* **PAMI-8**(6) pp. 679-698 (1986).

J P Changeux (Editor), *The Neural and Molecular Basis of Learning*, Wiley, New York (1987).

C K Chow and T Kaneko, Automatic Boundary Detection of the Left Ventricle from Cineangiograms, *Computers and Biomedical Research* **5**(4) pp. 388-410 (1972).

M B Clowes, On Seeing Things, *Artificial Intelligence* **2**(1) pp. 79-116 (1971).

R Davis and J King, An Overview of Production Systems, pp. 300-332 in *Machine Intelligence 8.* Ed. D Michie, Ellis Horwood, Chichester (1977).

P M Dew and L J Manning, Comparison of Systolic and SIMD Architectures for Computer Vision Computations, pp. 273-282 in *Systolic Arrays.* Hilger (1987).

P M Dew (Editor), *Proceedings of the International Conference on Parallel Processing for Computer Vision and Display (to appear).*

R O Duda and P E Hart, *Pattern Classification and Scene Analysis*, John Wiley and Sons, New York (1973).

T S Durrani, K Boyle, F Lotti, and A Rauf, Computer Aided Thermal Imaging Techniques for the Inspection of Composite Materials, in *Proceedings of the IEE Colloquium on Image Processing for Automated Inspection.* IEE, London (8th April 1986).

J A Feldman and Y Yakimovsky, Decision Theory and Artificial Intelligence, *Artificial Intelligence* **5** pp. 349-371 (1974).

R Fikes and T Kehler, The Role of Frame-based Representation in Reasoning, *Communications of the ACM* **28**(9) pp. 904-920 (1985).

M Fisz, *Probability Theory and Mathematical Statistics*, John Wiley and Sons, New York (1963).

J Foglein, K Paler, J Illingworth, and J Kittler, Local Ordered Grey levels as a Guide to Corner Detection, *Pattern Recognition* **17**(5) pp. 535-543 (1984).

J D Foley and A Van Dam, *Fundamentals of Interactive Computer Graphics*, Addison-Wesley, Reading, Massachusetts (1982).

D A Forsyth, A System for Finding Changes in Colour, in *Proceedings of the Third Alvey Vision Conference, Cambridge.* , Sheffield, England (September 1987).

W Frei and C C Chen, Fast Boundary Detection, a Generalization and a new Algorithm, *IEEE* **C-26** pp. 988-998 (October 1977).

Garibotto and Tosini, Description and Classification of 3D Objects, pp. 833-835 in *Proceedings of the 6th International Conference on Pattern Recognition (Munich).* IEEE, New York (1982).

C Goad, Special Purpose Automatic Programming for 3D model-based vision, pp. 94-104 in *Proceedings of the Image Understanding Workshop.* DARPA, Science Applications, Mclean, Va (1983).

R C Gonzalez and M G Thomason, *Syntactic Pattern Recognition: An Introduction*, Addison-Wesley, Reading, Massachusetts (1978).

R C Gonzalez and P Wintz, *Digital Image Processing (Second Edition)*, Addison Wesley, Reading, Massachusetts (1987).

R Gordon, G T Herman, and S A Johnson, Image Reconstruction from Projections, *Scientific American* **233**(4) pp. 56-71 (October 1975).

R L Gregory, *Eye and Brain*, McGraw Hill, New York (1978).

A Guzman, Decomposition of a Visual Scene into Three Dimensional Bodies, in *Automatic Interpretation and Classification of Images.* Ed. A Grasseli, Academic press, New York (1969).

Y Hara, N Akiyama, and K Karasaki, Automatic Inspection Systems for Printed Circuit Boards, *IEEE Transactions on Pattern Analysis and Machine Intelligence* **PAMI-5** pp. 623-630 (1983).

R M Haralick and L G Shapiro, The Consistent Labelling Problem, *IEEE Transactions on Pattern Analysis and Machine Intelligence* **PAMI-1**(2) pp. 173-184 (1979).

B K P Horn, Shape from Shading, in *The Psychology of Computer Vision.* Ed. P H Winston, McGraw-Hill, New York (1975).

P V C Hough, Method and Means for Recognizing Complex Patterns, US Patent 3069654 (1962).

T S Huang, G J Yang, and G Y Tang, A fast two dimensional median filtering algorithm, pp. 128-131 in *Proceedings of the IEEE Conference on Pattern Recognition and Image Processing.* (1978).

D A Huffman, Impossible Objects as Nonsense Sentences, in *Machine*

Intelligence 6. Ed. B Meltzer and D Michie, Edinburgh University Press (1971).

K Ikeuchi, Numerical Shape from Shading and Occluding Contours in a Single View, AI memo 566, MIT (February 1980).

K Ikeuchi and B K P Horn, Numerical Shape from Shading and Occluding Boundaries, *Artificial Intelligence* **17** pp. 141-184 (1981).

J Illingworth and J Kittler, Measures of Circularity for Automatic Inspection Applications, *Proceedings of the Society of Photo-Optical Instrumentation Engineers* **557** pp. 114-122 (1985).

J Illingworth and J Kittler, A Survey of Efficient Hough Transform Methods, in *Proceedings of the Third Alvey Vision Conference, Cambridge.* , Sheffield, England (September 1987).

P Jackson, *Introduction to Expert Systems*, Addison-Wesley, Reading, Massachusetts (1986).

R A Jarvis, A Perspective on Range Finding Technologies for Computer Vision, *IEEE Transactions on Pattern Analysis and Machine Intelligence* **PAMI-5**(2) pp. 122-139 (1983).

J Jelinek and P H Mowforth, Low Level Vision: Away from Edges, TIRM-84-003, The Turing Institute (December 1984).

S Kahan, T Pavlidis, and H S Baird, On the Recognition of Printed Characters of Any Font and Size, *IEEE Transactions on Pattern Analysis and Machine Intelligence* **PAMI-9**(2) pp. 274-286 (1987).

B Kani and M J Wilson, Adaptive Windows for Texture Discrimination, in *Proceedings of the Third Alvey Vision Conference, Cambridge.* , Sheffield, England (September 1987).

J R Kender, Shape from Texture: a brief Overview and a new Aggregation Transform, pp. 79-84 in *Proceedings of DARPA Image Understanding Workshop.* Carnegie Mellon University, Pittsburgh, PA (November 1978).

B W Kernighan and D M Ritchie, *The C Programming Language*, Prentice-Hall, Englewood Cliffs, New Jersey (1978).

T Kilvington, *Specification of Television Standards for 625-line System-l Transmissions*, BBC and ITA, London (January 1971).

C Kimme, D H Ballard, and J Sklansky, Finding Circles by an Array of Accumulators, *Communications of the ACM* **18**(2) pp. 120-122 (1975).

R A Kirsch, Computer determination of the constituent contours in a single view, *Computers and Biomedical research* **3**(4) pp. 315-328 (June 1971).

C A Kohl, A R Hanson, and E M Riseman, A goal-directed intermediate level executive for image interpretation, pp. 811-814 in *Proceedings 10th Int. Joint Conference on Artificial Intelligence.* IJCAI (1987).

E L J Leeuwenberg and H F J M Buffart, *Formal theories of visual perception*, John Wiley and Sons, New York (1978).

A Lev, S W Zucker, and A Rosenfeld, Iterative enhancement of Noisy Images, *IEEE Transactions on Systems, Man and Cybernetics* **SMC-7**(6) (June 1976).

H J Levesque, Knowledge Representation and Reasoning, pp. 255-287 in *Annual Review of Computer Science*. Ed. J F Traub et al., (1986).

D G Lowe, *Perceptual Organisation and Visual Recognition*, Kluwer-Nijhoff, Norwell, Massachusetts (1985).

A K Mackworth, Interpreting Pictures of Polyhedral Scenes, *Artificial Intelligence* **4**(2) pp. 121-137 (June 1973).

A K Mackworth, Consistency in Networks of Relations, *Artificial Intelligence* **8**(1) pp. 99-118 (1977).

D Marr, G Palm, and T Poggio, Analysis of a Cooperative Stereo Algorithm, *Biological Cybernetics* **28** pp. 223-229 (1978).

D Marr and T Poggio, A Computational Theory of Human Stereo Vision, *Proceedings of the Royal Society* **B 204** pp. 301-328 (1979).

D Marr and E Hildreth, Theory of Edge Detection, *Proceedings of the Royal Society* **B 207** pp. 187-217 (1980).

D Marr, *Vision*, Freeman, San Francisco (1982).

W S McCulloch and W H Pitts, A Logical Calculus Immanent in Nervous Activity, *Bull. Math. Biophys.* **5** pp. 115-133 (1943).

D J Meagher, Geometric Modelling using Octree Encoding, *Computer graphics Image processing* **19**(2) pp. 129-147 (June 1981).

L Miclet, *Structural Methods in Pattern Recognition*, North Oxford Academic, London (1986).

M Minsky, A Framework for Representing Knowledge, pp. 211-277 in *The Psychology of Computer Vision*. Ed. P H Winston, McGraw-Hill, New York (1975).

D T Morris and P Quarendon, An Algorithm for Direct Display of CSG Objects by Spatial Subdivision, in *NATO ASI F-17: Fundamental Algorithms for Computer Graphics*. Ed. R A Earnshaw, Springer-Verlag, Berlin (1985).

A Nazif, *A Rule-based Expert System for Image Segmentation (Ph.D. Thesis)*, McGill University, Montreal, Canada (1983).

A Nazif and M Levine, Low Level Image Segmentation: An Expert System, *IEEE Transactions on Pattern Analysis and Machine Intelligence* **PAMI-6**(5) pp. 555-577 (1984).

W Newman and R Sproull, *Principles of Interactive Computer Graphics*, McGraw-Hill, London (1979).

W Niblack, *Digital Image Processing*, Prentice Hall International (UK), Birkeroed, Denmark (1986).

N J Nilsson, *Principles of Artificial Intelligence*, Springer-Verlag, Berlin

(1982).

J A Noble, Finding Corners, in *Proceedings of the Third Alvey Vision Conference, Cambridge.* , Sheffield, England (September 1987).

Y Ohta, T Kanade, and T Sakai, A Production System for Region Analysis, pp. 684-686 in *Proceedings 6th Int. Joint Conference on Artificial Intelligence.* IJCAI (August 1979).

Y Ohta, *Knowledge Based Interpretation of Outdoor Natural Color scenes*, Pitman, London (1985).

D E Pearson, *Transmission and Display of Pictorial Information*, Pentech Press, London (1975).

S B Pollard, J E W Mayhew, and J P Frisby, PMF: A Stereo Correspondence Algorithm using a Disparity Gradient Limit, *Perception* **14** pp. 449-470 (1985).

J Porrill, S B Pollard, T P Pridmore, J B Bowen, J E W Mayhew, and J P Frisby, TINA: A 3D Vision System for Pick and Place, in *Proceedings of the Third Alvey Vision Conference, Cambridge.* , Sheffield, England (September 1987).

J M Prager, Extracting and Labeling Boundary Segments in Natural Scenes, *IEEE Transactions on Pattern Analysis and Machine Intelligence* **PAMI-2**(1) (1980).

W K Pratt, *Digital Image Processing*, Wiley Interscience, New York (1978).

J M S Prewitt, Object Enhancement and Extraction, in *Picture Processing and Psychopictorics*. Ed. B S Lipkin and A Rosenfeld, Academic Press, New York (1970).

A A G Requicha, Representations of Rigids: Theory, Methods and Systems, *ACM Computing Surveys* **12**(4) pp. 437-464 (December 1980).

A A G Requicha and H B Voelcker, *Solid Modelling - A Historical Summary and Contemporary Assessment*, Computer Graphics and Applications (1982).

L G Roberts, Machine Perception of Three Dimensional Solids, in *Optical and Electro-optical Information Processing*. Ed. J P Tipper et al., MIT Press, Cambridge, Massachusetts (1965).

F Hayes Roth, D A Waterman, and D B Lenat (Editors), *Building Expert Systems*, Addison Wesley, Reading, Massachusetts (1983).

B P D Ruff, A Pipelined Architecture for the Canny Edge Detector, in *Proceedings of the Third Alvey Vision Conference, Cambridge.* , Sheffield, England (September 1987).

D E Rumelhart and J L McClelland , *Parallel Distributed Processing (Volumes 1 & 2)*, MIT Press, Cambridge, Ma (1986).

B J Schafter, A Lev, S W Zucker, and A Rosenfeld, An Application of Relaxation Methods to Edge Reinforcement, *IEEE Transactions on Systems, Man and Cybernetics* **SMC-7** pp. 813-816 (November 1977).

R Shapira, A Technique for the Reconstruction of a Straight Edge, Wire Frame Object from two or more central Projections, *Computer Graphics and Image Processing* **4**(3) pp. 318-326 (December 1974).

L G Shapiro, Computer Vision Systems: Past, Present, Future, pp. 199-237 in *NATO ASI F-4: Pictorial Data Analysis*. Ed. R M Haralick, Springer-Verlag, Berlin (1983).

J C Simon, *Patterns and Operators: The Foundations of Data Representation*, North Oxford Academic, London (1986).

B I Soroka and R K Bajcsy, A Program for describing complex three dimensional Objects using Generalized Cylinders as Primitives, pp. 331-339 in *Proceedings of the Pattern Recognition and Image Processing Conference (Chicago)*. IEEE, New York (1978).

Spider, Spider Working Group, Joint Systems Development Corporation, Yuseigojyokai-Kotohira Building 14-1, 1-chome, Toranomon, Minato-ku, Tokyo 105, *Spider Users' Manual*, Yoshiaki Tanaka, Tokyo (December 1983).

T J Stonham, Practical Face Recognition and Verification with WISARD, Brunel University, Department of Electrical Engineering, Internal Report, Brunel University (1983).

T J Stonham, B A Wilkie, and L Masih, Higher Order Adaptive Networks - some Aspects of Multi-Class and Feedback Systems, in *Proceedings of the Third Alvey Vision Conference, Cambridge.* , Sheffield, England (September 1987).

P Swaminathan and S N Srihari, Document Image Binarization: Second Derivative Versus Adaptive Thresholding, Technical Report 86-02, Dept of Computer Science, University at Buffalo, Buffalo, New York (January 1986).

A M Tailor, D G Corr, A Cross, D C Hogg, D H Lawrence, D C Mason, and M Petrou, Knowledge-Based Segmentation for Remote-Sensing, in *Proceedings of the Third Alvey Vision Conference, Cambridge.* , Sheffield, England (September 1987).

S Tanimoto and T Pavlidis, A Hierarchical Data Structure for Picture Processing, *Computer Graphics and Image Processing* **4**(2) pp. 104-119 (June 1975).

M C Taylor, Verifying a Printed Circuit, Department of Computer Studies Report, University of Leeds, Leeds (1985).

J M Tenenbaum and H G Barrow, Experiments in Interpretation Guided Segmentation, *Artificial Intelligence* **8** pp. 241-274 (1977).

W V Thomas and C Connolly, Applications of Colour Processing in Optical Inspection, *Proceedings of the Society of Photo-Optical Instrumentation Engineers* **654** (**Automatic Optical Inspection**) pp. 116-122 (1986).

S Ullman, *The Interpretation of Visual Motion*, The MIT Press, Cambridge,

Massachusetts (1979).

D Waltz, Understanding Line Drawings of Scenes with Shadows, pp. 19-91 in *The Psychology of Computer Vision*. Ed. P H Winston, Mcgraw-Hill, New York (1975).

H Wang, Edge Detection in a New Dimension, University of Leeds, Department of Computer Studies, Technical Report, University of Leeds, Leeds, UK (1987).

D A Waterman, *A Guide to Expert Systems*, Addison-Wesley, Reading, Massachusetts (1986).

P H Winston, Learning Structural Descriptions From Examples (Ph.D Thesis), AI TR-231, MIT A.I. Laboratory, Cambridge, Massachusetts (1970).

P H Winston, Learning Structural Descriptions from Examples, in *The Psychology of Computer Vision*. Ed. P H Winston, McGraw Hill, New York (1975).

P H Winston, *Artificial Intelligence, Second Edition*, Addison-Wesley, Reading, Massachusetts (1984).

A P Witkin, Recovering Surface Shape and Orientation from Texture, *Artificial Intelligence* **17** pp. 17-45 (1981).

S W Zucker, Region Growing, Childhood and Adolescence, *Computer Graphics and Image Processing* **5**(3) pp. 382-399 (September 1976).

S W Zucker, R A Hummel, and A Rosenfeld, An Application of Relaxation Labeling to Line and Curve Enhancement, *IEEE Transactions on Computing* **C-26** pp. 394-403 (April 1977).

Bibliography

I Aleksander (Editor), *Artificial Vision for Robots*, Kogan Page, Southampton (1981).

D H Ballard and C M Brown, *Computer Vision*, Prentice Hall, New Jersey (1982).

B G Batchelor, Image Processing System Design, in *Automated Visual Inspection*. Ed. D C Hodgson, I F S (Publications) Ltd, Bedford UK (1985).

L Bolc (Editor), *Natural Language Communication with Pictorial Information Systems*, Springer-Verlag, Berlin (1984).

A Browne and L Norton-Wayne, *Vision and Information Processing for Automation*, Plenum, London (1986).

J P Changeux (Editor), *The Neural and Molecular Basis of Learning*, Wiley, New York (1987).

J B Deregowski, *Illusions, Patterns and Pictures: a Cross-Cultural Perspective*, Academic Press, London (1980).

J Dessimoz, Vision for Robots, in *Applications in AI*. Ed. S J Andriole, Petrocelli Books, Princeton, New Jersey (1985).

R C Gonzalez and P Wintz, *Digital Image Processing (Second Edition)*, Addison Wesley, Reading, Massachusetts (1987).

J S Griffith, *Mathematical Neurobiology*, Academic Press, London (1971).

W E L Grimson, *From Images to Surfaces*, The MIT Press, Cambridge, Massachusetts (1981).

E B Hunt, *Artificial Intelligence*, Academic Press, New York (1975).

J I Kahn and D H Foster, Horizontal-Vertical Structure in the Visual Comparison of Rigidly Transformed Patterns, *Journal of Experimental Psychology: Human Perception and Performance* 12 pp. 422-433 (1986).

T Kanade, A Theory of Origami World, *Artificial Intelligence* 13 pp. 279-311 (1980).

D G Lowe, *Perceptual Organisation and Visual Recognition*, Kluwer-Nijhoff, Norwell, Massachusetts (1985).

R Nevatia, *Machine Perception*, Prentice-Hall, Englewood Cliffs, New Jersey (1982).

T O'Shea (Editor), *Advances in Artificial Intelligence, Proc ECAI-84*, North-Holland, Oxford (1985%).

W K Pratt, *Digital Image Processing*, Wiley Interscience, New York (1978).

E M Riseman, *Computer Vision Systems*, Academic Press, London (1978).

C Ronse and P A Devijver, *Connected Components in Binary Images: the Detection Problem*, The Research Studies Press, Letchworth, Herts (1984).

A Rosenfeld (Editor), *Techniques for 3-D Machine Perception*, North-Holland, Oxford (1986).

R Salmon and M Slater, *Computer Graphics Systems and Concepts*, Addison-Wesley, Reading, Massachusetts (1987).

E C Schwab and H C Nusbaum (Editors), *Pattern Recognition by Humans and Machines*, Academic Press, London (1986).

S C Shapiro, *Techniques of Artificial Intelligence*, Van Nostrand, London (1979).

S Ullman, *The Interpretation of Visual Motion*, The MIT Press, Cambridge, Massachusetts (1979).

F J Varela, *Principles of Biological Autonomy*, North Holland, New York (1979).

P H Winston and B K P Horn, *LISP*, Addison Wesley, Reading, Massachusetts (1981).

Author Index

Authors (and co-authors) are indexed to the page on which reference to their work is made.

Index

Major entries are indicated by a **bold** page number.

205